the
BEATITUDES
and the
LORD'S
PRAYER

the BEATITUDES
and the
LORD'S
PRAYER

A.W. PINK

BAKER BOOK HOUSE
Grand Rapids, Michigan 49506

PHOTOLITHOPRINTED BY CUSHING - MALLOY, INC.
ANN ARBOR, MICHIGAN, UNITED STATES OF AMERICA

Contents

The Beatitudes

Introduction   9

1. The First Beatitude 15
   "Blessed are the poor in spirit: for theirs is the kingdom of
   heaven" (Matt. 5:3).

2. The Second Beatitude 17
   "Blessed are they that mourn: for they shall be comforted"
   (Matt. 5:4).

3. The Third Beatitude 23
   "Blessed are the meek: for they shall inherit the earth" (Matt.
   5:5).

4. The Fourth Beatitude 31
   "Blessed are they which do hunger and thirst after righteous-
   ness: for they shall be filled" (Matt. 5:6).

5. The Fifth Beatitude 37
   "Blessed are the merciful: for they shall obtain mercy" (Matt.
   5:7).

6. The Sixth Beatitude 43
   "Blessed are the pure in heart: for they shall see God" (Matt.
   5:8).

7. The Seventh Beatitude 49
   "Blessed are the peacemakers: for they shall be called the children of God" (Matt. 5:9).

8. The Eighth Beatitude 55
   "Blessed are they which are persecuted for righteousness' sake: for theirs is the kingdom of heaven. Blessed are ye, when men shall revile you, and persecute you, and shall say all manner of evil against you falsely, for my sake. Rejoice, and be exceeding glad: for great is your reward in heaven: for so persecuted they the prophets which were before you" (Matt. 5:10–12).

   Conclusion: The Beatitudes and Christ 61

The Lord's Prayer

Introduction 71

1. The Address 77
   "Our Father which art in heaven" (Matt. 6:9).

2. The First Petition 83
   "Hallowed be Thy name" (Matt. 6:9).

3. The Second Petition 91
   "Thy Kingdom come" (Matt. 6:10).

4. The Third Petition 99
   "Thy will be done in earth, as it is in heaven" (Matt. 6:10).

5. The Fourth Petition 105
   "Give us this day our daily bread" (Matt. 6:11).

6. The Fifth Petition 111
   "And forgive us our debts, as we forgive our debtors" (Matt. 6:12).

7. The Sixth Petition 117
   "And lead us not into temptation" (Matt. 6:13).

8. The Seventh Petition 123
   "But deliver us from evil" (Matt. 6:13).

9. The Doxology 129
   "For Thine is the Kingdom, and the power, and the glory, for ever. Amen" (Matt. 6:13).

The Beatitudes

Introduction

Opinion has been much divided concerning the design, scope, and application of the Sermon on the Mount. Most commentators have seen in it an exposition of Christian ethics. Men such as the late Count Tolstoi have regarded it as the setting forth of a "golden rule" for all men to live by. Others have dwelt upon its dispensational bearings, insisting that it belongs not to the saints of the present dispensation but to believers within a future millenium. Two inspired statements, however, reveal its true scope. In Matthew 5:1, 2, we learn that Christ was here teaching His disciples. From Matthew 7:28, 29, it is clear that He was also addressing a great multitude of the people. Thus it is evident that this address of our Lord contains instruction both for believers and unbelievers alike.

It needs to be borne in mind that this sermon was Christ's first utterance to the general public, who had

been reared in a defective Judaism. It was possibly His
first discourse to the disciples, too. His design was not
only to teach Christian ethics but to expose the errors of
Pharisaism and to awaken the consciences of His legalistic hearers. In Matthew 5:20 He said, "Except your
righteousness shall exceed the righteousness of the
scribes and Pharisees, ye shall in no case enter into the
Kingdom of heaven." Then, to the end of the chapter,
He expounded the spirituality of the Law so as to arouse
His hearers to see their need of His own perfect righteousness. It was their ignorance of the spirituality of
the Law that was the real source of Pharisaism, for its
leaders claimed to fulfill the Law in the *outward* letter.
It was therefore our Lord's good purpose to awaken their
consciences by enforcing the Law's true inner import
and requirement.

It is to be noted that this Sermon on the Mount is
recorded only in Matthew's Gospel. The differences between it and the Sermon on the Plain in Luke 6 are
pronounced and numerous. While it is true that
Matthew is by far the most Jewish of the four Gospels,
yet we believe it is a serious mistake to *limit* its application to godly Jews, either of the past or the future. The
opening verse of the Gospel, where Christ is presented
in a twofold way, should warn us against such a restric-
tion. There He is presented as Son of David and as Son
of Abraham, "the father of *all* them that believe" (Rom.
4:11). Therefore, we are fully assured that this sermon
enunciates spiritual principles that obtain in every age,
and on this basis we shall proceed.

Christ's first preaching seems to have been sum-

marized in one short but crucial sentence, like that of
John the Baptist before Him: "Repent ye: for the Kingdom of heaven is at hand" (Matt. 3:2; 4:17). It is not
appropriate in a brief study such as this to discuss that
most interesting topic, the Kingdom of heaven—what it
is and what the various periods of its development
are—but these Beatitudes teach us much about those
who *belong* to that Kingdom, and upon whom Christ
pronounced its highest forms of benediction.

Christ came once in the flesh, and He is coming yet
again. Each advent has a special object as connected with
the Kingdom of heaven. The first advent of our Lord was
for the purpose of establishing an empire among men
and over men, by laying the foundations of that empire
within individual souls. His second coming will be for
the purpose of setting up that empire in glory. It is therefore vitally important that we understand what the
character of the subjects in that Kingdom is, so that we
may know whether we belong to the Kingdom ourselves,
and whether its privileges, immunities, and future re-
wards are a part of our present and future inheritance.
Thus one may grasp the importance of a devout and
careful study of these Beatitudes. We must examine
them as a whole; we cannot take one alone without losing
a part of the lesson they jointly teach. These Beatitudes
form *one* portrait. When an artist draws a picture, each
line may be graceful and masterful, but it is the union of
the lines that reveals their mutual relation; it is the combination of the various artistic delineations and minute
touches that gives us the complete portrait. So here,
though each separate aspect has its own peculiar beauty

and grace and shows the hand of a master, it is only when we take all the lines in combination that we get the full portrait of a true subject and citizen in the Kingdom of God (Dr. A. T. Pierson paraphrased).

God's great salvation is free, "without money and without price" (Isa. 55:1). This is a most merciful provision of Divine grace, for were God to offer salvation for sale no poor sinner could secure it, seeing that he has *nothing* with which to purchase it. But the vast majority are insensible of this; yea, all of us are until the Holy Spirit opens our sin-blinded eyes. It is only those who have passed from death to life who become conscious of their poverty, take the place of beggars, are glad to receive Divine charity, and begin to seek the true riches. Thus "the *poor* have the Gospel preached to them" (Matt. 11:5), preached not only to their ears, but to their hearts!

Thus poverty of spirit, a consciousness of one's emptiness and need, results from the work of the Holy Spirit within the human heart. It issues from the painful discovery that all my righteousnesses are as filthy rags (Isa. 64:6). It follows my being awakened to the fact that my very best performances are unacceptable (yea, an abomination) to the thrice Holy One. Thus one who is *poor in spirit* realizes that he is a hell-deserving sinner.

Poverty of spirit may be viewed as the negative side of faith. It is that realization of one's utter worthlessness that precedes a laying hold of Christ by faith, a spiritual eating of His flesh and drinking of His blood (John 6:48–58). It is the work of the Spirit emptying the heart of self, that Christ may fill it. It is a sense of need and destitution. This first Beatitude, then, is foundational, describing a fundamental trait that is found in every regenerated soul. The one who is poor in spirit is nothing in his own eyes, and feels that his proper place is in the dust before God. He may, through false teaching or worldliness, leave that place, but God knows how to bring him back. And in His faithfulness and love He will do so, for the place of humble self-abasement before God is the place of blessing for His children. How to cultivate this God-honoring spirit is revealed by the Lord Jesus in Matthew 11:29.

He who is in possession of this poverty of spirit is pronounced *blessed:* because he now has a disposition that is the very reverse of that which was his by nature; because he possesses the first sure evidence that a Divine work of grace has been wrought within him; because such a spirit causes him to look outside of himself for true enrichment; because he is an heir of the Kingdom of heaven.

1

The First Beatitude

*"Blessed are the poor in spirit: for theirs is
the Kingdom of heaven"* (Matt. 5:3).

It is indeed blessed to mark how this sermon opens.
Christ began not by pronouncing maledictions on the
wicked, but by pronouncing benedictions on His people.
How like Him was this, to whom judgment is a strange
work (Isa. 28:21, 22; cf. John 1:17). But how strange is
the next word: "blessed" or "happy" are *the poor*—"the
poor in spirit." Who, previously, had ever regarded
them as the blessed ones of earth? And who, outside
believers, does so today? And how these opening words
strike the keynote of all Christ's subsequent teaching: it
is not what a man *does* but what he *is* that is most
important.

"Blessed are the poor in spirit." What is poverty of
spirit? It is the opposite of that haughty, self-assertive,
and self-sufficient disposition that the world so much
admires and praises. It is the very reverse of that inde-
pendent and defiant attitude that refuses to bow to God,

that determines to brave things out, and that says with Pharaoh, "Who is the Lord, that I should obey His voice?" (Exod. 5:2). To be *poor in spirit* is to realize that I have nothing, am nothing, and can do nothing, and have need of all things. Poverty of spirit is evident in a person when he is brought into the dust before God to acknowledge his utter helplessness. It is the first experiential evidence of a Divine work of grace within the soul, and corresponds to the initial awakening of the prodigal in the far country when he "began to be *in want*" (Luke 15:14).

2

The Second Beatitude

"Blessed are they that mourn, for they shall be comforted" (Matt. 5:4).

Mourning is hateful and irksome to poor human nature. From suffering and sadness our spirits instinctively shrink. By nature we seek the society of the cheerful and joyous. Our text presents an anomaly to the unregenerate, yet it is sweet music to the ears of God's elect. If "blessed," why do they "mourn"? If they "mourn," how can they be "blessed"? Only the child of God has the key to this paradox. The more we ponder our text the more we are constrained to exclaim, "Never man spake like this Man!" "Blessed [happy] are they that mourn" is an aphorism that is at complete variance with the world's logic. Men have in all places and in all ages regarded the prosperous and gay as the happy ones, but Christ pronounces happy those who are *poor* in spirit and who *mourn*.

Now it is obvious that it is not every species of mourning that is here referred to. There is a "sorrow of the

world [that] worketh death" (II Cor. 7:10). The mourning for which Christ promises comfort must be restricted
to that which is spiritual. The mourning that is blessed is
the result of a realization of God's holiness and goodness
that issues in a sense of the depravity of our natures and
the enormous guilt of our conduct. The mourning for
which Christ promises Divine comfort is a sorrowing
over our sins with a godly sorrow.

The eight Beatitudes are arranged in four pairs. Proof
of this will be furnished as we proceed. The first of the
series is the blessing that Christ pronounced upon those
who are poor in spirit, which we took as a description of
those who have been awakened to a sense of their own
nothingness and emptiness. Now the transition from
such poverty to mourning is easy to follow. In fact,
mourning follows so closely that it is in reality poverty's
companion.

The mourning that is here referred to is manifestly
more than that of bereavement, affliction, or loss. It is
mourning for sin.

> It is mourning over the felt destitution of our spiritual state,
> and over the iniquities that have separated us and God;
> mourning over the very morality in which we have boasted,
> and the self-righteousness in which we have trusted; sorrow
> for rebellion against God, and hostility to His will; and such
> mourning always goes side by side with conscious poverty
> of spirit (Dr. Pierson).

A striking illustration and exemplification of the spirit
upon which the Savior here pronounced His benediction
is to be found in Luke 18:9–14. There a vivid contrast is
presented to our view. First, we are shown a self-

righteous Pharisee looking up toward God and saying, "God, I thank Thee that I am not as other men are, extortioners, unjust, adulterers, or even as this publican. I fast twice in the week, I give tithes of all that I possess." This may all have been true as *he* looked at it, yet this man went down to his house in a state of condemnation. His fine garments were rags, his white robes were filthy, though he knew it not. Then we are shown the publican, standing afar off, who, in the language of the Psalmist, was so troubled by his iniquities that he was not able to look up (Ps. 40:12). He dared not so much as lift up his eyes to heaven, but smote upon his breast. Conscious of the fountain of corruption within, he cried, "God be merciful to me a sinner." *That* man went down to his house justified, because he was poor in spirit and mourned for sin.

Here, then, are the first birthmarks of the children of God. He who has never come to be poor in spirit and has never known what it is to really mourn for sin, though he belong to a church or be an officebearer in it, has neither seen nor entered the Kingdom of God. How thankful the Christian reader ought to be that the great God condescends to dwell in the humble and contrite heart! This is the wonderful promise made by God even in the Old Testament (by Him in whose sight the heavens are not clean, who cannot find in any temple that man has ever built for Him, however magnificent, a proper dwelling place—see Isa. 57:15 and 66:2)!

"Blessed are they that mourn." Though the primary reference is to that initial mourning commonly called *conviction of sin*, it is by no means to be limited to that.

Mourning is ever a characteristic of the normal Christian state. There is much that the believer has to mourn over. The plague of his own heart makes him cry, "O wretched man that I am" (Rom. 7:24). The unbelief that "doth so easily beset us" (Heb. 12:1) and sins that we commit, which are more in number than the hairs of our head, are a continual grief to us. The barrenness and unprofitableness of our lives make us sigh and cry. Our propensity to wander from Christ, our lack of communion with Him, and the shallowness of our love for Him cause us to hang our harps upon the willows. But there are many other causes for mourning that assail Christian hearts: on every hand hypocritical religion that has a form of godliness while denying the power thereof (II Tim. 3:5); the awful dishonor done to the truth of God by the false doctrines taught in countless pulpits; the divisions among the Lord's people; and strife between brethren. The combination of these provides occasion for continual sorrow of heart. The awful wickedness in the world, the despising of Christ, and untold human sufferings make us groan within ourselves. The closer the Christian lives to God, the more he will mourn over all that dishonors Him. This is the common experience of God's true people (Ps. 119:53; Jer. 13:17; 14:17; Ezek. 9:4).

"They shall be comforted." By these words Christ refers primarily to the removal of the guilt that burdens the conscience. This is accomplished by the Spirit's application of the Gospel of God's grace to one whom He has convicted of his dire need of a Savior. The result is a sense of free and full forgiveness through the merits of the atoning blood of Christ. This Divine comfort is "the peace of God, which passeth all understanding" (Phil. 4:7), filling the heart of the one who is now assured that he is "accepted in the Beloved" (Eph. 1:6). God wounds before healing, and abases before He exalts. First there is a revelation of His justice and holiness, then the making known of His mercy and grace.

The words "they shall be comforted" also receive a constant fulfillment in the experience of the Christian. Though he mourns his excuseless failures and confesses them to God, yet he is comforted by the assurance that the blood of Jesus Christ, God's Son, cleanses him from all sin (I John 1:7). Though he groans over the dishonor done to God on every side, yet is he comforted by the knowledge that the day is rapidly approaching when Satan shall be cast into hell forever and when the saints shall reign with the Lord Jesus in "new heavens and a new earth, wherein dwelleth righteousness" (II Peter 3:13). Though the chastening hand of the Lord is often laid upon him and though "no chastening for the present seemeth to be joyous, but grievous" (Heb. 12:11), nevertheless, he is consoled by the realization that this is all working out for him "a far more exceeding and eternal weight of glory" (II Cor. 4:17). Like the Apostle Paul, the believer who is in communion with his Lord can say, "As sorrowful, yet alway rejoicing" (II Cor. 6:10). He may often be called upon to drink of the bitter waters of Marah, but God has planted nearby a tree to sweeten them. Yes, *mourning* Christians are comforted even now by the Divine Comforter: by the ministrations of His servants, by encouraging words from fellow Christians, and (when these are not to hand) by the precious promises of the Word being brought home in power by the Spirit to their hearts out of the storehouse of their memories.

"They shall be comforted." The best wine is reserved for the last. "Weeping may endure for a night, but joy cometh in the morning" (Ps. 30:5). During the long night of His absence, believers have been called to fellowship with Him who was the Man of Sorrows. But it is written, "If . . . we suffer with Him . . . we [shall] be also glorified together" (Rom. 8:17). What comfort and joy will be ours when shall dawn the morning without clouds! Then "sorrow and sighing shall flee away" (Isa. 35:10). Then shall be fulfilled the words of the great heavenly voice in Revelation 21:3, 4:

> Behold, the tabernacle of God is with men, and He will dwell with them, and they shall be His people, and God Himself shall be with them, and be their God. And God shall wipe away all tears from their eyes; and there shall be no more death, neither sorrow, nor crying, neither shall there be any more pain: for the former things are passed away.

3

The Third Beatitude

*"Blessed are the meek: for they shall
inherit the earth"* (Matt. 5:5).

There have been considerable differences of opinion
as to the precise significance of the word *meek*. Some
regard its meaning as patience, a spirit of resignation;
some as unselfishness, a spirit of self-abnegation; others
as gentleness, a spirit of nonretaliation, bearing afflictions quietly. Doubtless, there is a measure of truth in
each of these definitions. Yet it appears to the writer that
they hardly go deep enough, for they fail to take note of
the *order* of this third Beatitude. Personally, we would
define meekness as humility. "Blessed are the meek,"
that is, the humble, the lowly. Let us see if other pas-
sages bear this out.

The first time the word *meek* occurs in Scripture is in
Numbers 12:3. Here the Spirit of God has pointed out a
contrast from that which is recorded in the previous
verses. There we read of Miriam and Aaron speaking
against Moses: "Hath the Lord indeed spoken *only* by

Moses? Hath He not spoken also *by us?*" Such language betrayed the pride and haughtiness of their hearts, their self-seeking and craving for honor. As the antithesis of this we read, "Now the man Moses was *very meek."* This must mean that he was actuated by a spirit the very opposite of the spirit of his brother and sister.

Moses was humble, lowly, and self-renouncing. This is recorded for our admiration and instruction in Hebrews 11:24–26. Moses turned his back on worldly honors and earthly riches, deliberately choosing the life of a pilgrim rather than that of a courtier. He chose the wilderness in preference to the palace. The humbleness of Moses is seen again when Jehovah first appeared to him in Midian and commissioned him to lead His people out of Egypt. "Who am *I,"* he said, "that *I* should go unto Pharaoh, and that *I* should bring forth the children of Israel out of Egypt?" (Exod. 3:11). What lowliness these words breathe! Yes, Moses was *very meek.*

Other Scripture texts bear out, and seem to necessitate, the definition suggested above. "The meek will He guide in judgment: and the meek will He teach His way" (Ps. 25:9). What can this mean but that the *humble* and *lowly-hearted* are the ones whom God promises to counsel and instruct? "Behold, thy King cometh unto thee, meek, and sitting upon an ass" (Matt. 21:5). Here is meekness or lowliness incarnate. "Brethren, if a man be overtaken in a fault, ye which are spiritual, restore such an one in the spirit of meekness; considering thyself, lest thou also be tempted" (Gal. 6:1). Is it not plain that this means that a spirit of *humility* is required in him who would be used of God in restoring an erring brother? We are to learn of Christ, who was "meek and lowly in heart." The latter term explains the former. Note that they are linked together again in Ephesians 4:2, where the order is "lowliness and meekness." Here the order is deliberately reversed from that in Matthew 11:29. This shows us that they are synonymous terms.

Having thus sought to establish that meekness, in the *Scriptures,* signified *humility and lowliness,* let us now note how this is further borne out by the context and then endeavor to determine the manner in which such meekness finds expression. It must be steadily kept in mind that in these Beatitudes our Lord is describing the orderly development of God's work of grace as it is experientially realized in the soul. First, there is poverty of spirit: a sense of my insufficiency and nothingness. Next, there is mourning over my lost condition and sorrowing over the awfulness of my sins against God. Following this, in order of spiritual experience, is humbleness of soul.

The one in whom the Spirit of God has worked, producing a sense of nothingness and of need, is now brought into the dust before God. Speaking as one whom God used in the ministry of the Gospel, the Apostle Paul said, "The weapons of our warfare are not carnal, but mighty through God to the pulling down of strong holds; Casting down imaginations, and every high thing that exalteth itself against the knowledge of God, and bringing into captivity every thought to the obedience of Christ" (II Cor. 10:4, 5). The *weapons* that the apostles used were the searching, condemning, humbling truths of Scripture. These, as applied effectually by the Spirit, were mighty to the pulling down of strongholds, that is, the powerful prejudices and self-righteous defenses within which sinful men took refuge. The results are the same today: proud *imaginations* or reasonings—the enmity of the carnal mind and the opposition of the newly regenerate mind concerning salvation is now brought into captivity to the obedience of Christ.

By nature every sinner is Pharisaical, desiring to be justified by the works of the Law. By nature we all inherit from our first parents the tendency to manufacture for ourselves a covering to hide our shame. By nature every member of the human race walks in the way of Cain, who sought to find acceptance with God on the ground of an offering produced by his own labors. In a word, we desire to gain a standing before God on the basis of personal merits; we wish to purchase salvation by our good deeds; we are anxious to win heaven by our own doings. God's way of salvation is too humbling to suit the carnal mind, for it removes all ground for *boasting.* It is therefore unacceptable to the proud heart of the unregenerate.

Man wants to have a hand in his salvation. To be told that God will receive nought from him, that salvation is solely a matter of Divine mercy, that eternal life is only for those who come empty-handed to receive it solely as a matter of *charity,* is offensive to the self-righteous religionist. But not so to the one who is poor in spirit and who mourns over his vile and wretched state. The very word *mercy* is music to his ears. Eternal life as God's free gift suits his poverty-stricken condition. Grace—the sovereign favor of God to the hell-deserving—is just what he feels he must have! Such a one no longer has any thought of justifying himself in his own eyes; all his haughty objections against God's benevolence are now silenced. He is glad to own himself a beggar and bow in the dust before God. Once, like Naaman, he rebelled against the humbling terms announced by God's servant; but now, like Naaman at the end, he is glad to dismount from his chariot of pride and take his place in the dust before the Lord.

It was when Naaman bowed before the humbling word of God's servant that he was healed of his leprosy. In the same way, when the sinner owns his worthlessness, Divine favor is shown to him. Such a one receives the Divine benediction: "*Blessed* are the *meek.*" Speaking anticipatively through Isaiah, the Savior said, "The Lord hath anointed Me to preach good tidings unto the meek" (Isa. 61:1). And again it is written, "For the Lord taketh pleasure in His people: He will beautify the meek with salvation" (Ps. 149:4).

While humility of soul in bowing to God's way of salvation is the primary application of the third Beatitude, it must not be limited to that. *Meekness* is also an intrinsic aspect of the "fruit of the Spirit" that is wrought in and produced through the Christian (Gal. 5:22, 23). It is that quality of spirit that is found in one who has been schooled to mildness by discipline and suffering and brought into sweet resignation to the will of God. When in exercise, it is that grace in the believer that causes him to bear patiently insults and injuries, that makes him ready to be instructed and admonished by the least eminent of saints, that leads him to esteem others more

highly than himself (Phil. 2:3), and that teaches him to
ascribe all that is good in himself to the sovereign grace
of God.

On the other hand, true *meekness* is not weakness. A
striking proof of this is furnished in Acts 16:35–37. The
apostles had been wrongfully beaten and cast into
prison. On the next day the magistrates gave orders for
their release, but Paul said to their agents, "Let them
come themselves and fetch us out." God-given meekness
can stand up for God-given rights. When one of the
officers smote our Lord, He answered, "If I have spoken
evil, bear witness of the evil: but if well, why smitest
thou Me?" (John 18:23).

The spirit of meekness was perfectly exemplified only
by the Lord Jesus Christ, who was "meek and lowly in
heart." In His people this blessed spirit fluctuates, often-
times beclouded by risings up of the flesh. Of Moses it is
said, "They provoked his spirit, so that he spake unad-
visedly with his lips" (Ps. 106:33). Ezekiel says of himself: "I went in bitterness, in the heat of my spirit; but
the hand of the Lord was strong upon me" (Ezek. 3:14).
Of Jonah, after his miraculous deliverance, we read: "It
displeased Jonah exceedingly, and he was very angry"
(Jonah 4:1). Even the humble Barnabas parted from Paul
in a bitter temper (Acts 15:37–39). What warnings are
these! How much we need to learn of Christ!

"Blessed are the meek: for they shall inherit the
earth." Our Lord was alluding to, and applying, Psalm
37:11. The promise seems to have both a literal and
spiritual meaning: "The meek shall inherit the earth; and
shall delight themselves in the abundance of peace." The

meek are those who have the greatest enjoyment of the good things of the present life. Delivered from a greedy and grasping spirit, they are content with such things as they have. "A little that a righteous man hath is better than the riches of many wicked" (Ps. 37:16). Contentment of mind is one of the fruits of meekness of spirit. The proud and restless do not "inherit the earth," though they may own many acres of it. The humble Christian has far more enjoyment in a cottage than the wicked has in a palace. "Better is little with the fear of the Lord than great treasure and trouble therewith" (Prov. 15:16).

"The meek shall inherit the earth." As we have said, this third Beatitude is an allusion to Psalm 37:11. Most probably the Lord Jesus was using Old Testament language to express New Covenant truth. The *flesh* and *blood* of John 6:50–58 and the *water* of John 3:5 have, to the regenerate, a *spiritual* meaning; so here with the word *earth* or *land*. Both in Hebrew and in Greek, the principal terms rendered by our English words *earth* and *land* may be translated either literally or spiritually, depending upon the context.

His words, literally understood, are, "they shall inherit the land," i.e., Canaan, "the land of promise." He speaks of the blessings of the new economy in the language of Old Testament prophecy. Israel according to the flesh (the external people of God under the former economy) were a figure of Israel according to the spirit (the spiritual people of God under the new economy); and Canaan, the [earthly] inheritance of the former, is the type of that aggregate of heavenly and spiritual blessings which form the inheritance of the latter. To "inherit the land" is to enjoy the peculiar blessings of the people of God under the new economy; it is

to become heirs of the world, heirs of God and joint-heirs
with Christ [Rom. 8:17]. It is to be "blessed... with all
spiritual blessings in the heavenlies in Christ" [Eph. 1:3],
to enjoy that true peace and rest of which Israel's in Canaan
was a figure (Dr. John Brown).

No doubt there is also reference to the fact that the meek
shall ultimately inherit the "new earth, wherein
dwelleth righteousness" (II Peter 3:13).

4

The Fourth Beatitude

"Blessed are they which do hunger and thirst after righteousness: for they shall be filled" (Matt. 5:6).

In the first three Beatitudes we are called upon to witness the heart exercises of one who has been awakened by the Spirit of God. First, there is a sense of need, a realization of my nothingness and emptiness. Second, there is a judging of self, a consciousness of my guilt, and a sorrowing over my lost condition. Third, there is a cessation of seeking to justify myself before God, an abandonment of all pretenses to personal merit, and a taking of my place in the dust before God. Here, in the fourth Beatitude, the eye of the soul is turned away from self toward God for a very special reason: there is a longing after a righteousness that I urgently need but know that I do not possess.

There has been much needless quibbling as to the precise import of the word *righteousness* in our present text. The best way to ascertain its significance is to go back to the Old Testament Scriptures where this term is

31

used, and then to shine upon these the brighter light
furnished by the New Testament Epistles.

"Drop down, ye heavens, from above, and let the
skies pour down *righteousness:* let the earth open, and
let them bring forth *salvation,* and let righteousness
spring up together; I the Lord have created it" (Isa.
45:8). The first half of this verse refers, in figurative language, to the advent of Christ to this earth; the second
half to His resurrection, when He was "raised again for
our justification" (Rom. 4:25). "Hearken unto Me, ye
stouthearted, that are far from righteousness: I bring
near *My righteousness;* it shall not be far off, and *My
salvation* shall not tarry: and I will place salvation in Zion
for Israel My glory" (Isa. 46:12, 13). "*My righteousness* is
near; *My salvation* is gone forth, and Mine arms shall
judge the people; the isles shall wait upon Me, and on
Mine arm shall they trust" (Isa. 51:5). "Thus saith the
Lord, Keep ye judgment, and do justice: for *My salvation* is near to come, and *My righteousness* to be revealed" (Isa. 56:1). "I will greatly rejoice in the Lord, my
soul shall be joyful in my God; for He hath clothed me
with the garments of *salvation,* He hath covered me
with the robe of *righteousness*" (Isa. 61:10a). These pas-
sages make it clear that God's *righteousness* is synonymous with God's *salvation.*

The Scriptures cited above are unfolded in Paul's
Epistle to the Romans, where the Gospel receives its
fullest exposition. In Romans 1:16, 17a, Paul says, "For I
am not ashamed of the Gospel of Christ: for it is the
power of God unto *salvation* to every one that believeth;
to the Jew first, and also to the Greek. For therein is the

righteousness of God revealed from faith to faith." In Romans 3:22–24 we read, "Even the righteousness of God which is by faith of Jesus Christ unto all and upon all them that believe: for there is no difference: For all have sinned, and come short of the glory of God; Being justified freely by His grace through the redemption that is in Christ Jesus." In Romans 5:19, this blessed declaration is made: "For as by one man's disobedience many were made [legally constituted] sinners, so by the obedience of One shall many be made [legally constituted] righteous." In Romans 10:4, we learn that "Christ is the end of the Law *for righteousness* to every one that believeth."

The sinner is destitute of righteousness, for "there is none righteous, no, not one" (Rom. 3:10). God has, therefore, provided in Christ a *perfect righteousness* for each and all of His people. This righteousness, this satisfying of all the demands of God's holy Law against us, was worked out by our Substitute and Surety. This righteousness is now *imputed* to (that is, legally credited to the account of) the believing sinner. Just as the sins of God's people were all transferred to Christ, so His righteousness is placed upon them (II Cor. 5:21). These few words are but a brief summary of the teaching of Scripture on this vital and blessed subject of the perfect righteousness that God requires of us and that is ours by faith in the Lord Christ.

"Blessed are they which do hunger and thirst after righteousness." Hungering and thirsting expresses vehement desire, of which the soul is acutely conscious. First, the Holy Spirit brings before the heart the holy

requirements of God. He reveals to us His perfect standard, which He can never lower. He reminds us that
"except your righteousness shall exceed the righteousness of the scribes and Pharisees, ye shall in no case
enter into the Kingdom of heaven" (Matt. 5:20). Second,
the trembling soul, conscious of his own abject poverty
and realizing his utter inability to measure up to God's
requirements, sees no help in himself. This painful discovery causes him to mourn and groan. Have *you* done
so? Third, the Holy Spirit then creates in the heart a
deep "hunger and thirst" that causes the convicted sinner to look for relief and to seek a supply *outside* of
himself. The believing eye is then directed to Christ,
who is "THE LORD OUR RIGHTEOUSNESS" (Jer.
23:6).

Like the previous ones, this fourth Beatitude describes a twofold experience. It obviously refers to the
initial hungering and thirsting that occurs before a sinner
turns to Christ by faith. But it also refers to the continual
longing that is perpetuated in the heart of every saved
sinner until his dying day. Repeated exercises of this
grace are felt at varying intervals. The one who longed to
be saved *by* Christ, now yearns to be made *like* Him.
Looked at in its widest aspect, this hungering and thirsting refers to a panting of the renewed heart after God
(Ps. 42:1), a yearning for a closer walk with Him, and a
longing for more perfect conformity to the image of His
Son. It tells of those aspirations of the new nature for
Divine blessing that alone can strengthen, sustain, and
satisfy.

Our text presents such a paradox that it is evident that

no carnal mind ever invented it. Can one who has been brought into vital union with Him who is the Bread of Life and in whom all fullness dwells be found *still* hungering and thirsting? Yes, such is the experience of the renewed heart. Mark carefully the tense of the verb: it is not "Blessed are they *which have* hungered and thirsted," but "Blessed are they *which do* hunger and thirst." Do you, dear reader? Or are you *content* with your attainments and satisfied with your condition? Hungering and thirsting after righteousness has always been the experience of God's true saints (Phil. 3:8–14).

"They shall be filled." Like the first part of our text, this also has a double fulfillment, both initial and continuous. When God creates a hunger and a thirst in the soul, it is so that *He* may satisfy them. When the poor sinner is made to feel his need for Christ, it is to the end that he may be drawn to Christ and led to embrace Him as his only righteousness before a holy God. He is delighted to confess Christ as his new-found righteousness and to glory in Him alone (I Cor. 1:30, 31). Such a one, whom God now calls a "saint" (I Cor. 1:2; II Cor. 1:1; Eph. 1:1; Phil. 1:1), is to experience an ongoing *filling:* not with wine, wherein is excess, but with the Spirit (Eph. 5:18). He is to be *filled* with the peace of God that passeth all understanding (Phil. 4:7). We who are trusting in the righteousness of Christ shall one day be *filled* with Divine blessing without any admixture of sorrow; we shall be *filled* with praise and thanksgiving to Him who wrought every work of love and obedience in us (Phil. 2:12, 13) as the visible fruit of His saving work in and for us. In this world, "He hath *filled* the hungry with good things" (Luke 1:53) such as this world can neither give to nor withhold from those who "seek the Lord (Ps. 34:10). He bestows such goodness and mercy upon us, who are the sheep of His pasture, that our cups run over (Ps. 23:5, 6). Yet all that we presently enjoy is but a mere foretaste of all that our "God hath prepared for them that love Him" (I Cor. 2:9). In the eternal state, we will be *filled* with perfect holiness, for "we shall be like Him" (I John 3:2). Then we shall be done with sin forever. Then we shall "hunger *no more*, neither thirst *any more.*"

5

The Fifth Beatitude

"Blessed are the merciful: for they shall obtain mercy" (Matt. 5:7).

In the first four Beatitudes, which have already been considered, a definite progression of spiritual awakening and transformation has been noted as one of the thrusts of our Lord's teaching. First, there is a discovery of the fact that I am nothing, have nothing, and can do nothing—poverty of spirit. Second, there is conviction of sin, a consciousness of guilt producing godly sorrow—mourning. Third, there is a renouncing of self-dependence and a taking of my place in the dust before God—meekness. Fourth, there follows an intense longing after Christ and His salvation—hungering and thirsting after righteousness. But, in a sense, all of this is simply *negative*, for it is the believing sinner's perception of what is defective in himself and a yearning for what is desirable. In the next four Beatitudes we come to the manifestation of *positive good* in the believer, the fruits of a new creation and the blessings of a transformed character. How this shows us, once more, the importance of noting that order in which God's truth is presented to us!

"Blessed are the merciful: for they shall obtain mercy." How grossly has this text been perverted by merit-mongers! Those who insist that the Bible teaches salvation by works appeal to this verse in support of their pernicious error. But nothing could be less to their purpose. Our Lord's purpose is not to set forth the foundation upon which the sinner's hope of mercy from God must rest, but rather it is to describe the character of His genuine disciples. *Mercifulness* is a prominent trait in this character. According to our Lord's teaching, mercy is an essential feature of that holy character to which God has inseparably connected the enjoyment of His own sovereign kindness. Thus, there is nothing whatever in this verse that favors the erroneous teachings of Roman Catholicism.

The position occupied by this Beatitude in its context is another key to its interpretation. The first four describe the initial exercises of heart in one who has been awakened by the Holy Spirit. In the preceding verse, the soul is seen hungering and thirsting after Christ, and then filled by Him. Here we are shown the first effects and evidences of this filling. Having obtained mercy of the Lord, the saved sinner now exercises mercy. It is not that God requires us to be merciful in order that we might be entitled to His mercy, for that would overthrow the whole scheme of Divine grace! But having been the recipient of His wondrous mercy, I cannot help but now act mercifully toward others.

What is *mercifulness?* It is a gracious disposition toward my fellow creatures and fellow Christians. It is that kindness and benevolence that feels the miseries of others. It is a spirit that regards with compassion the sufferings of the afflicted. It is that grace that causes one to deal leniently with an offender and to scorn the taking of revenge.

> It is the forgiving spirit; it is the non-retaliating spirit; it is the spirit that gives up all attempt at self-vindication and would not return an injury for an injury, but rather good in the place of evil and love in the place of hatred. That is mercifulness. Mercy being received by the forgiven soul, *that* soul comes to appreciate the beauty of mercy, and yearns to exercise toward other offenders similar grace to that which is exercised towards one's self (Dr. A. T. Pierson).

The source of this merciful temper is not to be attributed to anything in our fallen human nature. It is true that there are some who make no profession of being Christians in whom we often see not a little of kindliness of disposition, sympathy for the suffering, and a readiness to forgive those who have wronged them. Admirable as this may be, from a purely human viewpoint, it falls far below that mercifulness upon which Christ here pronounced His benediction. The amiability of the flesh has no spiritual value, for its movements are neither regulated by the Scriptures nor exercised with any reference to the Divine authority. The mercifulness of this fifth Beatitude is that spontaneous outflow of a heart that is captivated by, and in love with, the mercy of God.

The mercifulness of our text is the product of the new nature implanted by the Holy Spirit in the child of God.

It is called into exercise when we contemplate the wondrous grace, pity, and longsuffering of God toward such
unworthy wretches as ourselves. The more I ponder
God's sovereign mercy to me, the more I shall think of
the unquenchable fire from which I have been delivered
through the sufferings of the Lord Jesus. The more conscious I am of my indebtedness to Divine grace, the
more mercifully I shall act toward those who wrong,
injure, and hate me.

Mercifulness is one of the attributes of the spiritual
nature that one receives at the new birth. Mercifulness
in the child of God is but a reflection of the abundant
mercy that is found in his heavenly Parent. Mercifulness
is one of the natural and necessary consequences of a
merciful Christ indwelling us. It may not always be exercised; it may at times be stifled or checked by fleshly
indulgence. But when the general tenor of a Christian's
character and the main trend of his life are taken into
account, it is clear that mercifulness is an unmistakable
trait of the new man. "The wicked borroweth, and
payeth not again; but the righteous sheweth mercy, and
giveth" (Ps. 37:21). It was *mercy* in Abraham, after he
had been wronged by his nephew, that caused him to
pursue and secure the deliverance of Lot (Gen. 14:1–16).
It was *mercy* on the part of Joseph, after his brethren had
so grievously mistreated him, that caused him to freely
forgive them (Gen. 50:15–21). It was *mercy* in Moses,
after Miriam had rebelled against him and the Lord had
smitten her with leprosy, that caused him to cry, "Heal
her now, O God, I beseech Thee" (Num. 12:13). It was
mercy that caused David to spare the life of his enemy

Saul when that wicked king was in his hands (I Sam. 24:1–22; 26:1–25). In sad and striking contrast, of Judas it is said that he "remembered not to shew mercy, but persecuted the poor and needy man" (Ps. 109:16).

In Romans 12:8 the Apostle Paul gives vital instruction concerning *the spirit* in which mercy is to be exercised: "he that showeth mercy" is to do so "with *cheerfulness.*" The direct reference here is to the giving of money for the support of poor brethren, but this loving principle really applies to *all* compassion shown to the afflicted. Mercy is to be exercised cheerfully, to demonstrate that it is not only done voluntarily but that it is also a pleasure. This spares the feelings of the one helped, and soothes the sorrows of the sufferer. It is this quality of *cheerfulness* that gives most value to the service rendered. The Greek word is most expressive, denoting joyful eagerness, a gladsome affability that makes the visitor like a sunbeam, warming the heart of the afflicted. Since Scripture tells us that "God loveth a cheerful giver" (II Cor. 9:7), we may be sure that the Lord takes note of the spirit in which we respond to His admonitions.

"For they shall obtain mercy." These words enunciate a principle or law that God has ordained in His government over our lives here on earth. It is summarized in that well-known word: "Whatsoever a man soweth, that shall he also reap" (Gal. 6:7b). The Christian who is merciful in his dealings with others will receive merciful treatment at the hands of his fellows; for "with what measure ye meet, it shall be measured to you again" (Matt. 7:2). Therefore it is written, "He that followeth after righteousness and mercy findeth life, righteous-

ness, and honour" (Prov. 21:21). The one who shows
mercy to others gains personally thereby: "The merciful
man doeth good to his own soul" (Prov. 11:17a). There is
an inward satisfaction in the exercise of benevolence and
pity to which the highest gratification of the selfish man
is not to be compared. "He that hath mercy on the poor,
happy is he" (Prov. 14:21b). The exercise of mercy is a
source of satisfaction to God Himself: "He *delighteth* in
mercy" (Mic. 7:18). So must it be to us.

"For they shall obtain mercy." Not only does the merciful Christian gain by the happiness that accrues to his
own soul through the exercise of this grace, not only will
the Lord, in His overruling providence, make his mercifulness return again to him at the hands of his fellow
men, but the Christian will also obtain mercy *from God.*
This truth David declared: "With the merciful Thou wilt
shew Thyself merciful" (Ps. 18:25). On the other hand,
the Savior admonished His disciples with these words:
"But if ye forgive not men their trespasses, neither will
your Father forgive your trespasses" (Matt. 6:15).

"For they shall obtain mercy." Like the promises attached to the previous Beatitudes, this one also looks
forward to the future for its final fulfillment. In II
Timothy 1:16, 18, we find the Apostle Paul writing, "The
Lord give mercy unto the house of Onesiphorus. . . . The
Lord grant unto him that he may find mercy of the Lord
in that day." In Jude 21, the saints are also exhorted to
be "looking for the *mercy* of our Lord Jesus Christ"—this
refers to the ultimate acknowledgement of us as His own
redeemed people at His second coming in glory.

6

The Sixth Beatitude

*"Blessed are the pure in heart: for they
shall see God"* (Matt. 5:8).

This is another of the Beatitudes that has been grossly
perverted by the enemies of the Lord, enemies who
have, like their predecessors the Pharisees, posed as the
champions of the truth and boasted of a sanctity superior
to that which the true people of God would dare to
claim. All through this Christian era, also, there have
been poor, deluded souls who have claimed an entire
purification of the old man. Others have insisted that
God has so completely renewed them that the carnal
nature has been eradicated, so that they not only commit
no sins but have no sinful desires or thoughts. But the
Spirit-inspired Apostle John declares, "If we say that we
have [present tense] no sin, we deceive ourselves, and
the truth is not in us" (I John 1:8). Of course, such people
appeal to the Scriptures in support of their vain delusion,
applying to *experience* verses that describe the *legal* bene-
fits of the Atonement. The words "and the blood of Jesus

Christ His Son cleanseth us from all sin" (I John 1:7) do
not mean that our hearts have been washed from every
trace of the corrupting defilements of evil, but primarily
teach that the sacrifice of Christ has availed for the judi-
cial blotting out of sins. When the Apostle Paul, describing the man who is a new creature in Christ, says that
"old things are passed away; behold, all things are become new" (II Cor. 5:17), he is speaking of the new disposition of the Christian's *heart*, which is wholly unlike
his inner disposition prior to the Holy Spirit's work of
regeneration.

That *purity of heart* does not mean sinlessness of life
is clear from the inspired record of the history of God's
saints. Noah got drunk; Abraham equivocated; Moses
disobeyed God; Job cursed the day of his birth; Elijah
fled in terror from Jezebel; Peter denied Christ. "Yes,"
perhaps someone will exclaim, "but all these things
transpired before Christianity was established!" True,
but it has also been the same since then. Where shall we
go to find a Christian of superior attainments to those of
the Apostle Paul? And what was his experience? Read
Romans 7 and see. When he would do good, evil was
present with him (v. 21). There was a law in his members, warring against the law of his mind, and bringing
him into captivity to the law of sin that was in his members (v. 23). He did, with the mind, serve the Law of
God; nevertheless, with the flesh he served the law of sin
(v. 25). The truth is that one of the most conclusive
evidences that we *do* possess a pure heart is the discovery and consciousness of the remaining *impurity* that

continues to plague our hearts. But let us come closer to our text.

"Blessed are the pure in heart." In seeking an interpretation to any part of this Sermon on the Mount, the first thing to bear in mind is that those whom our Lord was addressing had been reared in Judaism. As one said who was deeply taught of the Spirit,

> I cannot help thinking that our Lord, in using the terms before us, had a tacit reference to that character of external sanctity or purity which belonged to the Jewish people, and to that privilege of intercourse with God which was connected with that character. They were a people separated from the nations polluted with idolatry; set apart as holy to Jehovah; and, as a holy people, they were permitted to draw near to their God, the only living and true God, in the ordinances of His worship. On the possession of this character, and on the enjoyment of this privilege, the Jewish people plumed themselves.
>
> A higher character, however, and a higher privilege, belonged to those who should be the subjects of the Messiah's reign. They should not only be externally holy, but "pure in heart"; and they should not merely be allowed to approach towards the holy place, where God's honour dwelt, but they should "see God," be introduced into the most intimate intercourse with Him. Thus viewed, as a description of the spiritual character and privileges of the subjects of the Messiah *in contrast* with the external character and privileges of the Jewish people, the passage before us is full of the most important and interesting truth (Dr. John Brown).

"Blessed are the pure in heart." Opinion is divided as to whether these words of Christ refer to the *new heart* received at regeneration or to that moral *transformation of character* that results from a Divine work of grace having been wrought in the soul. Probably both aspects of the truth are combined here. In view of the late place that this Beatitude occupies in the series, it would appear that the purity of heart upon which our Savior pronounced His blessing is that internal cleansing that both accompanies and follows the new birth. Thus, inasmuch as no inward purity exists in the natural man, that purity attributed by Christ to the godly man must be traced back, as to its beginnings, to the Spirit's sovereign work of regeneration.

The Psalmist said, "Behold, Thou desirest truth in the inward parts: and in the hidden part Thou shalt make me to know wisdom" (Ps. 51:6). This spiritual purity that God demands penetrates far beyond the mere outward renovations and reformations that comprise such a large part of the efforts now being put forth in Christendom! Much that we see around us is a *hand* religion—seeking salvation by works—or a *head* religion that rests satisfied with an orthodox creed. But God "looketh on the heart" (I Sam. 16:7), that is, He looks upon the whole inner being, including the understanding, the affections, and the will. It is because God looks within that He must give a "*new* heart" (Ezek. 36:26) to His own people and *blessed* indeed are they who have received such, for it is a *pure heart* that is acceptable to the Giver.

As intimated above, we believe that this sixth Beatitude contemplates both the new heart received at regeneration and the transformation of character that follows God's work of grace in the soul. First, there is a "washing of regeneration" (Titus 3:5), by which we understand a cleansing of the affections, which are now subsequently set upon things above, instead of things below. This is closely linked with that change that follows upon the heels of regeneration, in which all believers undergo a "purifying [of] their hearts by faith" (Acts 15:9). Accompanying this is the cleaning of the conscience (Heb. 10:22), which refers to the removal of the burden of conscious guilt. This results in the inward realization that, "being justified by faith, we have peace with God through our Lord Jesus Christ" (Rom. 5:1).

But the purity of heart commended here by Christ goes further than this. What is *purity?* It is freedom from defilement and divided affections; it is sincerity, genuineness, and singleness of heart. As a quality of Christian character, we would define it as *godly simplicity*. It is the opposite of subtlety and duplicity. Genuine Christianity lays aside not only malice, but guile and hypocrisy also. It is not enough to be pure in words and in outward deportment. Purity of desires, motives, and intents is what should (and does in the main) characterize the child of God. Here, then, is a most important test for every professing Christian to apply to himself. Are my affections set upon things above? Are my motives pure? Why do I assemble with the Lord's people? Is it to be seen of men, or is it to meet with the Lord and to enjoy sweet communion with Him and His people?

"For they shall see God." Once more we would point out that the promises attached to these Beatitudes have both a present and a future fulfillment. The pure in heart possess spiritual discernment, and with the eyes of their

understanding they obtain clear views of the Divine
character and perceive the excellency of His attributes.
When the eye is single the whole body is full of light.

> In the truth, the faith of which purifies the heart, they "see
> God"; for what is that truth, but a manifestation of the glory
> of God in the face of Jesus Christ [II Cor. 4:6]—an illustri-
> ous display of the combined radiance of Divine holiness and
> Divine benignity!... And he [who is pure in heart] not
> only obtains clear and satisfactory views of the Divine
> character, but he enjoys intimate and delightful commu-
> nion with God. He is brought very near God: God's mind
> becomes his mind; God's will becomes his will; and his
> fellowship is truly with the Father and with His Son Jesus
> Christ.
>
> They who are pure in heart "see God" in this way, even
> in the present world; and in the future state their knowl-
> edge of God will become far more extensive and their fel-
> lowship with Him far more intimate; for though, when
> compared with the privileges of a former dispensation,
> even now as with open face we behold the glory of the Lord
> [II Cor. 3:18], yet, in reference to the privileges of a higher
> economy, we yet see but through a glass darkly—we know
> but in part, we enjoy but in part. But that which is in part
> shall be done away, and that which is perfect shall come.
> We shall yet see face to face and know even as we are known
> (I Cor. 13:9–12); or to borrow the words of the Psalmist,
> we shall behold His face in righteousness, and shall be sat-
> isfied when we awake in His likeness (Ps. 17:15). Then,
> and not till then, will the full meaning of these words be
> understood, that the pure in heart shall see God (Dr. John
> Brown).

7

The Seventh Beatitude

"Blessed are the peacemakers: for they shall be called the children of God" (Matt. 5:9).

This seventh Beatitude is the hardest of all to expound. The difficulty lies in determining the precise significance and scope of the word *peacemakers*. The Lord Jesus does not say, "Blessed are the peacelovers," or "Blessed are the peace-keepers," but "Blessed are the peacemakers." Now it is apparent on the surface that what we have here is something more excellent than that love of concord and harmony, that hatred of strife and turmoil, that is sometimes found in the natural man, because the peacemakers that are here in view shall be called *the children of God*. Three things must guide us in seeking the true interpretation: (1) the character of those to whom our Lord was speaking; (2) the place occupied by our text in the series of Beatitudes; and (3) its connection with the Beatitude that follows.

The Jews, in general, regarded the Gentile nations with bitter contempt and hatred, and they expected that, under

49

the Messiah, there should be an uninterrupted series of warlike attacks made on these nations, till they were completely destroyed or subjugated to the chosen people of God [an idea based, no doubt, on what they read in the Book of Joshua concerning the experiences of their forefathers]. In their estimation, those emphatically deserved the appellation of "happy" who should be employed under Messiah the Prince to avenge on the heathen nations all the wrongs these had done to Israel. How different is the spirit of the new economy! How beautifully does it accord with the angelic anthem which celebrated the nativity of its Founder: "Glory to God in the highest, and on earth peace, good will toward men!" (Dr. John Brown).

This seventh Beatitude has to do more with conduct than character, though, of necessity, there must first be a peaceable spirit before there will be active efforts put forth to make peace. Let it be remembered that in this first section of the Sermon on the Mount, the Lord Jesus is defining the character of those who are subjects and citizens in His Kingdom. First, He describes them in terms of the initial experiences of those in whom a Divine work is wrought. The first four Beatitudes, as has been previously stated, may be grouped together as setting forth the negative graces of their hearts. Christ's subjects are not self-sufficient, but consciously poor in spirit. They are not self-satisfied, but mourning because of their spiritual state. They are not self-important, not lowly or meek. They are not self-righteous, but hungering and thirsting for the righteousness of Another. In the next three Beatitudes, the Lord names their positive graces. Having tasted of the mercy of God, they are merciful in their dealings with others. Having received from the Spirit a spiritual nature, their eye is single to behold the glory of God. Having entered into the peace that Christ made by the blood of His cross, they are now anxious to be used by Him in bringing others to the enjoyment of such peace.

That which helps us, perhaps as much as anything else, to fix the meaning of this seventh Beatitude is the link that exists between it and the one that immediately follows. In our previous chapters, we have called attention to the fact that the Beatitudes are obviously grouped together in pairs. Poverty of spirit is always accompanied by mourning, as is meekness or lowliness by hungering and thirsting after the righteousness of God. Mercifulness toward men is united to purity of heart towards God, and peacemaking is coupled with being persecuted for righteousness' sake. Thus verses 10–12 supply us with the key to verse 9.

By approaching the seventh Beatitude from each of the three separate viewpoints mentioned above, we arrive at the same conclusion. First, let us consider the marked contrast between the tasks that God assigned to His people under the Old Covenant and New Covenant respectively. After the giving of the Law, Israel was commanded to take up the sword and to conquer the land of Canaan, *destroying* the enemies of Jehovah. The risen Christ has given different orders to His Church. Throughout this Gospel dispensation, we are to go into all nations as heralds of the cross, *seeking the reconciliation* of those who by nature are at enmity with our Master. Second, this grace of *peacemaking* supplements the six graces mentioned in the previous verses. Perhaps the fact that this is the *seventh* Beatitude indicates that it was our Lord's intent to teach that it is this attribute that gives *completeness* or wholeness to Christian character. We must certainly conclude that it is an unspeakable privilege to be sent forth as ambassadors of peace. Furthermore, those who fancy themselves to be Christians, yet have no interest in the salvation of fellow sinners, are self-deceived. They possess a defective Christianity, and have no right to expect to share in the blessed inheritance of the children of God. Third, there is a definite link between this matter of our being *peacemakers* and the persecution to which our Master alludes in verses 10–12. By mentioning these two aspects of Christian character and experience side by side in His discourse, Christ is teaching that the opposition encountered by His disciples in the path of duty is the result of their faithfulness in the service to which they have been called. Thus we may be certain that the *peacemaking* of our text refers primarily to our being instruments in God's hands for the purpose of reconciling to Him those who are actively engaged in warfare against Him (cf. John 15:17–27).

We have dealt at some length on the reasons that have led us to conclude that the *peacemakers* referred to in our text are those who beseech sinners to be reconciled to God (II Cor. 5:20), because most of the commentators are very unsatisfactory in their expositions. They see in this Beatitude nothing more than a blessing pronounced by Christ on those who endeavor to promote unity, to heal breaches, and to restore those who are estranged. While we fully agree that this is a most blessed exercise, and that the Christian is, by virtue of his being indwelt by Christ, a lover of peace and concord, yet we do not believe that this is what our Lord had in mind here.

The believer in Christ knows that there is no peace for the wicked. Therefore, he earnestly desires that they should acquaint themselves with God and be at peace (Job 22:21). Believers know that peace with God is only *through our Lord Jesus Christ* (Col. 1:19, 20). For this reason we speak of Him to our fellow men as the Holy Spirit leads us to do so. Our feet are "shod with the preparation of the Gospel of peace" (Eph. 6:15); thus we are equipped to testify to others concerning the grace of God. Of us it is said, "How beautiful are the feet of them that preach the Gospel of *peace,* and bring glad tidings of good things!" (Rom. 10:15). All such are pronounced *blessed* by our Lord. They cannot but be blessed. Next to the enjoyment of peace in our own souls must be our delight in bringing others also (by God's grace) to enter into this peace. In its wider application, this word of Christ may also refer to that spirit in His followers that delights to pour oil upon the troubled waters, that aims to right wrongs, that seeks to restore kindly relations by dealing with and removing difficulties and by neutralizing and silencing acrimonies.

"Blessed are the peacemakers: for they shall be called the children of God." The word *called* here seems to mean "acknowledged as." God shall *own* them as His own children.

He is "the God of peace" (Heb. 13:20). His great object, in the wonderful scheme of redemption, is to "gather together in one all things in Christ," whether they be things "in heaven," or things "on earth" (Eph. 1:10). And all those who, under the influence of Christian truth, are peacemakers show that they are animated with the same principle of action as God, and as "obedient children" [I Peter 1:14] are cooperating with Him in His benevolent design (Dr. John Brown).

The world may despise them as fanatics, professors of religion may regard them as narrow-minded sectarians, and their relatives may look upon them as fools. But the great God owns them as His children even now, distinguishing them by tokens of His peculiar regard and causing His Spirit within them to witness to them that they are sons of God. But in the Day to come, He will publicly avow His relationship to them in the presence of an assembled universe. However humble their present situation in life may be, however despised and misrepresented by their fellow men, they shall yet "shine forth as the sun in the Kingdom of their Father" (Matt. 13:43). Then shall transpire the glorious and long-awaited "*manifestation* of the sons of God" (Rom. 8:19).

8

The Eighth Beatitude

*"Blessed are they which are persecuted for righteousness'
sake: for theirs is the Kingdom of heaven. Blessed are ye,
when men shall revile you, and persecute you, and shall
say all manner of evil against you falsely, for My sake.
Rejoice, and be exceeding glad: for great is your reward
in heaven: for so persecuted they the prophets which
were before you"* (Matt. 5:10–12).

The Christian life is full of strange paradoxes that are
quite insoluble to human reason, but that are easily understood by the spiritual mind. God's saints rejoice with
joy unspeakable, yet they also mourn with a lamentation
to which the worldling is an utter stranger. The believer
in Christ has been brought into contact with a source of
vital satisfaction that is capable of meeting every longing,
yet he pants with a yearning like that of a thirsty heart
(Ps. 42:1). He sings and makes melody in his heart to the

Lord, yet he groans deeply and daily. His experience is often painful and perplexing, yet he would not part with it for all the gold in the world. These puzzling paradoxes are among the evidences he possesses that he is indeed blessed of God. Such are the thoughts evoked by our present text. Who, by mere reasoning, would ever conclude that the reviled, the persecuted, the defamed, are *blessed?*

> It is a strong proof of human depravity that men's curses and Christ's blessings should meet on the same persons. Who would have thought that a man could be persecuted and reviled, and have all manner of evil said of him, for righteousness' sake? And do wicked men really hate justice and love those who defraud and wrong their neighbours? No; they do not dislike righteousness as it respects *themselves:* it is only that species of it which respects *God* and religion that excites their hatred. If Christians were content with doing justly and loving mercy, and would cease walking humbly with God [Mic. 6:8], they might go through the world, not only in peace, but with applause; but he that will *live godly* in Christ Jesus shall suffer persecution (II Tim. 3:12). Such a life reproves the ungodliness of men and provokes their resentment (Andrew Fuller).

Verses 10–12 plainly go together and form the eighth and last Beatitude of this series. It pronounces a double blessing upon a double line of conduct. This at once suggests that it is to be looked at in a twofold way. What we have in verse 10 is to be regarded as an *appendix* to the whole series, describing the experience that will surely be met with by those whose character Christ has described in the previous verses. The carnal mind is enmity against God (Rom. 8:7), and the more His children are conformed to His image the more they will bring down upon themselves the spite of His foes. Being "persecuted for righteousness' sake" means being opposed because of right living. Those who perform their Christian duty condemn those who live to please self, and therefore evoke their hatred. This persecution assumes various forms, from annoying and taunting to oppressing and tormenting.

Verses 10–12 contain a supplementary word to the seventh Beatitude. That which arouses the anger of Satan and most stirs up his children are the efforts of Christians to be peacemakers. The Lord here prepares us to expect that loyalty to Him and His Gospel will result in our own peace being disturbed, introducing us to the prospect of strife and warfare. Proof of this is found when He says, "For *so* persecuted they the *prophets* which were before you." It is *service for God* that calls forth the fiercest opposition. Necessarily so, for we are living in a world that is hostile to Christ, as His cross has once and for all demonstrated.

Our Lord mentions, in verse 11, three sorts of suffering that His disciples should expect to endure in the line of duty. The first is *reviling,* that is, verbal abuse or vituperation. The second is *persecution.* This word is a proper rendering of a Greek word meaning "to pursue," which means, in this case, "to harass, trouble, or molest" (either physically or verbally). It may include the sort of *handling* or *hunting down* to which Saul of Tarsus subjected the Church before he was apprehended by Christ (Acts 8, 9). Christ sets forth the third type of suffering as follows: "Blessed are ye, when men... *shall say all manner of evil against you falsely....*" Thus He de-

scribes the defamation of character to which His saints
must be subjected. This last is doubly painful to sensitive
temperaments, finding its realization in the countless
calumnies that the Devil is never weary of inventing in
order to intensify the sufferings of the children of God.
The words "persecuted for righteousness' sake" and "for
My sake" caution us to see to it that we are opposed and
hated *solely* because we are the followers of the Lord
Jesus, and not on account of our own misconduct or
injudicious behavior (see I Peter 2:19-24).

Persecution has ever been the lot of God's people.
Cain slew Abel. "And wherefore slew he him? Because
his own works were evil, and his brother's righteous"
(I John 3:12). Joseph was persecuted by his brethren, and
down in Egypt he was cast into prison for righteousness'
sake (Gen. 37, 39). Moses was reviled again and again
(see Exod. 5:21; 14:11; 16:2; 17:2; etc.). Samuel was rejected (I Sam. 8:5). Elijah was despised (I Kings 18:17)
and persecuted (I Kings 19:2). Micaiah was hated (I Kings
22:8). Nehemiah was oppressed and defamed (Neh. 4).
The Savior Himself, the faithful Witness of God, was
put to death by the people to whom He ministered.
Stephen was stoned, Peter and John cast into prison,
James beheaded, while the entire course of the Apostle
Paul's Christian life and ministry was one long series of
bitter and relentless persecutions.

It is true that the persecution of the saints today is in a
much milder form than it assumed in other ages. Nevertheless, it is just as real. Through the goodness of God
we have long been protected from legal persecution, but
the enmity of Satan finds other ways and means of ex-

pressing itself. Let persecuted Christians remember this comforting truth: "For unto you it is *given* in the behalf of Christ, not only to believe on Him, but also *to suffer* for His sake" (Phil. 1:29). The words of Christ in John 15:19, 20, have never been repealed:

> If ye were of the world, the world would love his own: but because ye are not of the world, but I have chosen you out of the world, therefore the world hateth you. Remember the word that I said unto you, The servant is not greater than his lord. If they have persecuted Me, they will also persecute you; if they have kept My saying, they will keep yours also.

The world's hatred manifests itself in derision, reproach, slander, and ostracism. May Divine grace enable us to heed this word: "But if, when ye do well, and suffer for it, yet take it *patiently*, this is acceptable with God" (I Peter 2:20).

The Lord Jesus here pronounced *blessed* or happy those who, through devotion to Him, would be called upon to suffer. They are *blessed* because such are given the unspeakable privilege of having fellowship in the sufferings of the Savior (Phil. 3:10). They are *blessed* because such "tribulation worketh patience; And patience, experience; and experience, hope: And hope maketh not ashamed" (Rom. 5:3-5). They are *blessed* because they shall be fully recompensed in the great Day to come. Here is rich comfort indeed. Let not the soldier of the cross be dismayed because the fiery darts of the wicked one are hurled against him. Rather let him gird on more firmly the Divinely provided armor. Let not the child of God become discouraged because his efforts to please Christ make some of those who call themselves Christians speak evil of him. Let not the Christian imagine that fiery trials are an evidence of God's disapproval.

"Rejoice, and be exceeding glad." Not only are the afflictions that faithfulness to Christ involves to be patiently endured, but they are to be received with joy and gladness. This we should do for three reasons. (1) These afflictions come upon us for Christ's sake; and since He suffered so much for our redemption, we ought to rejoice greatly when we are called upon to suffer a little for Him. (2) These trials bring us into fellowship with a noble company of martyrs, for to meet with afflictions associates us with the holy prophets and apostles. In such company, reproach becomes praise and dishonor turns to glory. (3) We who suffer persecution for Christ's sake are promised a great reward in heaven. Verily, we may rejoice, however fierce the present conflict may be. Having deliberately chosen to suffer with Christ rather than enjoy the pleasures of sin for a season (Heb. 11:25), we shall also reign with Him, according to His own sure promise (Rom. 8:17). Remember Peter and John, who "departed from the presence of the council, *rejoicing* that they were counted worthy to suffer shame for His name" (Acts 5:41). So, too, Paul and Silas, in the Philippian dungeon and with backs bleeding, "sang praises unto God" (Acts 16:25). We are told that others "took joyfully the spoiling of [their] goods," knowing in themselves that they had "in heaven a better and an enduring substance" (Heb. 10:34). May Divine grace enable all maligned, misunderstood, and oppressed saints of God to draw from these precious words of Christ that comfort and strength that they need.

Conclusion

The Beatitudes and Christ

Our meditations upon the Beatitudes would not be complete unless they turned our thoughts to the Person of our blessed Lord. As we have endeavored to show, they describe the character and conduct of a Christian. Since Christian character is formed in us by the experiential process of our being conformed to the image of God's Son, then we must turn our gaze upon Him who is the perfect pattern. In the Lord Jesus Christ we find the brightest manifestations and the highest exemplifications of all the various spiritual graces that are found (as dim reflections) in His followers. Not one or two but all of these perfections were displayed by Him, for He is not only *lovely*, but "altogether *lovely*" (Song of Sol. 5:16). May the Holy Spirit, who is here to glorify Him, take now of the things of Christ and show them unto us (John 16:14, 15).

First let us consider the words, "Blessed are the poor in spirit." How marvelous it is to see how the Scriptures speak of Him who was rich becoming poor for our sakes, that we through His poverty might be rich (II Cor. 8:9). Great indeed was the poverty into which He entered. Born of parents who were poor in this world's goods, He commenced His earthly life in a manger. During His youth and early manhood, He toiled at the carpenter's bench. After His public ministry had begun, He declared that though the foxes had their holes and the birds of the air their nests, the Son of Man had not where to lay His head (Luke 9:58). If we trace out the Messianic utterances recorded in the Psalms by the Spirit of prophecy, we shall find that again and again He confessed to God His poverty of spirit: "I am poor and sorrowful" (Ps. 69:29); "Bow down Thine ear, O Lord, hear Me: for I am poor and needy" (Ps. 86:1); "For I am poor and needy, and My heart is wounded within Me" (Ps. 109:22).

Second, let us ponder the words, "Blessed are they that mourn." Christ was indeed the chief Mourner. Old Testament prophecy contemplated Him as "a Man of *Sorrows*, and acquainted with *grief*" (Isa. 53:3). When contending with the Pharisees over their slavish observance of the Sabbath, and while seeking to teach them, by precept and example, a proper understanding of God's holy institution, He "grieved for the hardness of their hearts" (Mark 3:5). Behold Him *sighing* before He healed the deaf and dumb man (Mark 7:34). Mark Him weeping by the graveside of Lazarus (John 11:35). Hear His lamentation over the beloved city: "O Jerusalem, Jerusalem . . . how often would I have gathered thy children together" (Matt. 23:37). Draw near and reverently behold Him in the gloom of Gethsemane, pouring out His petitions to the Father "with strong crying and tears" (Heb. 5:7). Bow down in awe and wonder as you hear Him crying from the cross, "My God, My God, Why hast Thou forsaken Me?" (Mark 15:34). Hearken to His plaintive plea, "Is it nothing to you, all ye that pass by? behold, and see if there be any sorrow like unto My sorrow" (Lam. 1:12).

Third, behold the beauty of Christ in the saying, "Blessed are the meek." A score of examples might be drawn from the Gospels that illustrate the lovely lowliness of the incarnate Lord of glory. Mark it in the men selected by Him to be His ambassadors. He chose not the wise, the learned, the great, or the noble. At least four of them were fishermen, and one was in the employment of the Roman government as a despised tax collector. Witness His lowliness in the company that He kept. He sought not the rich and renowned, but was "a friend of publicans and sinners" (Matt. 11:19). See it in the miracles that He wrought. Again and again He enjoined the healed to go and tell no man what had been done for them. Behold it in the unobtrusiveness of His service. Unlike the hypocrites, who sounded a trumpet before them when they were about to bestow alms on some poor person, He sought not the limelight, but shunned advertising and disdained popularity. When the crowds would make Him their idol, He avoided them (Mark 1:45; 7:24). "When Jesus therefore perceived that they would come and take Him by force, to make Him a king, He departed again into a mountain Himself alone" (John 6:15). When His brethren urged

Him, saying, "Shew Thyself to the world," He declined and went up to the feast in secret (John 7:2–10). When He, in fulfillment of prophecy, presented Himself to Israel as their King, He entered Jerusalem in a most lowly fashion, riding upon the foal of an ass (Zech. 9:9; John 12:14).

Fourth, consider how these words are best exemplified in Christ: "Blessed are they which do hunger and thirst after righteousness." What a summary this is of the inner life of the man Christ Jesus! Before the Incarnation, the Holy Spirit announced, "And righteousness shall be the girdle of His loins" (Isa. 11:5). When Christ entered this world, He said, "Lo, I come to do Thy will, O God" (Heb. 10:9). As a boy of twelve He asked, "Wist ye not that I must be about My Father's business?" (Luke 2:49). At the beginning of His public ministry He declared, "Think not that I am come to destroy the law, or the prophets: I am not come to destroy, but to fulfill" (Matt. 5:17). To His disciples He declared, "My meat is to do the will of Him that sent Me, and to finish His work" (John 4:34). Of Him the Holy Spirit has said, "Thou lovest righteousness, and hatest wickedness: therefore God, Thy God, hath anointed Thee with the oil of gladness above Thy fellows" (Ps. 45:7). Well may He be called "THE LORD OUR RIGHTEOUSNESS" (Jer. 23:6).

Fifth, note the words, "Blessed are the merciful." In Christ we see mercy personified. It was mercy to poor lost sinners that caused the Son of God to exchange the glory of heaven for the shame of earth. It was wondrous and matchless mercy that took Him to the cross, there to be made a curse for His people. So, it is "not by works of righteousness which we have done, but according to His mercy [that] He saved us" (Titus 3:5). He is, even now, exercising mercy on our behalf as our "merciful and faithful High Priest" (Heb. 2:17). So also we are continually to be "looking for the mercy of our Lord Jesus Christ unto eternal life" (Jude 21), because He will show mercy in the Day of Judgment to all who believe upon Him (II Tim. 1:18).

Sixth, contemplate the words, "Blessed are the pure in heart." This, too, was perfectly exemplified in Christ. He was the "Lamb without blemish and without spot" (I Peter 1:19). In becoming man, He was uncontaminated, contracting none of the defilements of sin. His humanity was, and is, perfectly *holy* (Luke 1:35). He was "holy, harmless, undefiled, separate from sinners" (Heb. 7:26). "In Him is no sin" (I John 3:5). Therefore, He "did no sin" (I Peter 2:22) and "knew no sin" (II Cor. 5:21). "He is pure" (I John 3:3). Because He was absolutely pure in nature, His motives and actions were always pure. When He said, "I seek not Mine own glory" (John 8:50), He summed up the whole of His earthly career.

Seventh, ponder the words, "Blessed are the peacemakers." Supremely true is this of our blessed Savior. He is the One who "made peace through the blood of His cross" (Col. 1:20). He was appointed to be a *propitiation* (Rom. 3:25), that is, the One who would appease God's wrath, satisfying every demand of His broken Law, and glorifying His justice and holiness. He has also made peace between Jews and Gentiles (Eph. 2:11–18). Even now Christ Jesus is seated in majesty upon the throne of His father David (Acts 2:29–36), reigning as the "Prince of Peace. Of the increase of His government and peace there shall be no end, upon the throne of David" (Isa. 9:6, 7). When Christ returns to raise the dead and to judge the world in righteousness, then He shall purge this war-torn earth of sin and of all the effects of the Fall (Rom. 8:19–23). We may look confidently to that time when the Lord Christ shall thus restore peace in the "new heavens and a new earth, wherein dwelleth righteousness" (II Peter 3:13).

Eighth, meditate on these words: "Blessed are they which are persecuted for righteousness' sake." None was ever persecuted as was the Righteous One, as may be seen by the symbolic reference to Him in Revelation 12:4! By the Spirit of prophecy He declared, "I am afflicted and ready to die from My youth up" (Ps. 88:15). At the beginning of His ministry, when Jesus was teaching in Nazareth (His home town), the people "rose up, and thrust Him out of the city, and led Him unto the brow of the hill whereon their city was built, that they might cast Him down headlong" (Luke 4:29). In the temple precincts, leaders of the Jews "took up stones to cast at Him" (John 8:59). All through His ministry His steps were dogged by enemies. The religious leaders charged Him with having a demon (John 8:48). Those who sat in the gate spoke against Him, and He was the song of the drunkards (Ps. 69:12). At His trial they plucked off His hair (Isa. 50:6), spat in His face, buffeted Him, and smote Him with the palms of their hands (Matt. 26:67). After He was scourged by the soldiers and crowned with thorns, He was led carrying His own cross to Calvary, where they crucified Him. Even in His dying hours He was not left in peace, but was persecuted by revilings and scoffings. How unutterably mild, by comparison, is the persecution that we are called upon to endure for His sake!

In like manner, each of the *promises* attached to the Beatitudes finds its accomplishment in Christ. Poor in spirit He was, and His supremely is the Kingdom. Mourn He did, yet He will be comforted as He sees of the travail of His soul (Isa. 53:11). He was meekness personified, yet He is now seated upon a throne of glory. He hungered and thirsted after righteousness, yet now He is filled with satisfaction as He beholds that the righteousness which He worked out has been imputed to His people. Pure in heart, He sees God as none other sees Him (Matt. 11:27). As the Peacemaker, He is acknowledged as the unique Son of God by all the blood-bought children. As the persecuted One, great is His reward, for He has been given the name above all others (Phil. 2:9–11). May the Spirit of God occupy us more and more with Him who is fairer than the children of men (Ps. 45:2).

The Lord's Prayer

Introduction

After all that has been spoken and written by godly men on *prayer*, we need something better than that which is of mere human origin to guide us if we are to perform aright this essential duty. How ignorant and sinful creatures are to endeavor to come before the Most High God, how they are to pray acceptably to Him and to obtain from Him what they need, can be discovered only as the great Hearer of prayer is pleased to reveal His will to us. This He *has* done: (1) by opening up a new and living way of access into His immediate presence for the very chief of sinners; (2) by appointing prayer as the chief means of intercourse and blessing between Himself and His people; and (3) by graciously supplying a *perfect pattern* after which the prayers of His people are to be modeled. Note the wise instruction of the Westminster divines: "The whole Word of God is of use to direct us in prayer, but the special rule of direction is that form of prayer which Christ taught His disciples, commonly called *The Lord's Prayer*" (*The Westminster Shorter Catechism*).

From earliest times it has been called "the Lord's Prayer," not because it is one that He Himself addressed to the Father, but because it was graciously furnished by Him to teach us both the *manner and method* of how to pray and the *matters* for which to pray. It should therefore be highly esteemed by Christians. Christ knew both our needs and the Father's good will toward us, and thus He has mercifully supplied us with a simple yet comprehensive directory. Every part or aspect of prayer is included therein. Adoration is found in its opening clauses and thanksgiving in the conclusion. Confession is necessarily implied, for that which is asked for supposes our weakness or sinfulness. Petitions furnish the main substance, as in all praying. Intercession and supplication on behalf of the glory of God and for the triumph of His Kingdom and revealed will are involved in the first three petitions, whereas the last four are concerned with supplication and intercession concerning our own personal needs and those of others, as is indicated by pronouns in the plural number.

This prayer is found twice in the New Testament, being given by Christ on two different occasions. This, no doubt, is a hint for preachers to reiterate that which is of fundamental importance. The variations are significant. The language of Matthew 6:9 intimates that this prayer is given to us for a *model*, yet the words of Luke 11:2 indicate that it is to be used by us as a *form*. Like everything in Scripture, this prayer is perfect—perfect in its order, construction, and wording. Its order is adoration, supplication, and argumentation. Its petitions are seven in number. It is virtually an epitome of the Psalms and a most excellent summary of all prayer. Every clause in it occurs in the Old Testament, denoting that our prayers must be Scriptural if they are to be acceptable. "And this is the confidence that we have in Him, that, if we ask any thing according to His will, He heareth us" (I John 5:14). But we cannot know His will if we are ignorant of His Word.

It has been alleged that this prayer was designed only for the temporary use of Christ's first disciples, until such time as the New Covenant was inaugurated. But both Matthew and Luke wrote their Gospels years *after* the Christian dispensation had commenced, and neither of them gives any intimation that it had become obsolete and no longer of service to Christians. It is contended by some that this prayer is not suitable for believers now, inasmuch as the petitions in it are not offered in the name of Christ, and contain no express reference to His atonement and intercession. But this is a serious misconception and mistake; for by parity of reasoning, none of the Old Testament prayers, indeed none of the Psalms, could be used by us! But the prayers of Old Testament believers were presented to God *for His name's sake;* and Christ was the Angel of the Covenant of whom it was said, *"My name is in Him"* (Exod. 23:20, 21). Not only is the Lord's Prayer to be offered in reliance upon Christ's mediation, but it is that which He specially directs and authorizes us to offer.

In more recent times, certain "students of prophecy"

have objected to the use of this prayer on dispensational grounds, arguing that it is exclusively a Jewish prayer and legalistic in its tenor. But this is nothing more nor less than a blatant attempt of Satan to rob God's children of a valuable portion of their birthright. Christ did not give this prayer to Jews as Jews, but to His *disciples*. It is addressed to "Our Father," and is therefore to be used by all the members of His family. It is recorded not only in Matthew but also in Luke, the *Gentile* Gospel. Christ's injunction, after His resurrection, for His disciples to teach believers to observe all things *whatsoever* He had commanded them (Matt. 28:20) includes His commandment in Matthew 6:9-13. There is nothing whatever in this prayer *unsuited* to the Christian today, and everything in it is needed by him.

It has long been a matter of dispute, which has given rise to much acrimonious controversy, whether the Lord's Prayer is to be regarded as a form to be used or a pattern to be imitated. The right answer to this question is that it is to be considered as *both*. In Matthew it is manifestly brought forward as an example or pattern of the kind of prayer that is to be offered under the new economy. "After this manner therefore pray ye." We are to pray "with that reverence, humility, seriousness, confidence in God, concern for His glory, love to mankind, submission, moderation in temporal things, and earnestness about spiritual things which it inculcates" (Thomas Scott). But in Luke 11:2 we find our Lord teaching this: "When ye pray, *say* . . . ," that is, we are to use His words as a formula. It is, then, the duty of Christ's disciples in their praying both to use the Lord's Prayer continually as a pattern and sometimes as a form.

As for those who object to the using of any *form* of prayer, let us remind them that God Himself often puts into the mouths of His needy people the very language that they are to employ in approaching Him. For example, the Lord says to Israel, "Take with you *words*, and turn to the Lord: *say* unto Him, Take away all iniquity, and receive us graciously" (Hos. 14:2). Doubtless, we need to be much on our guard against merely *formal*, and still more so against a *superstitious*, observance of the Lord's Prayer. Nevertheless, we must as sedulously avoid going to the opposite extreme and never employing it at all. In the opinion of this writer, it ought to be reverently and feelingly recited once at every public service and used daily at family worship. That it has been perverted by some, whose too frequent use thereof seems to amount to the "vain repetitions" that the Savior prohibited (Matt. 6:7), is no valid reason why we should be altogether deprived of offering it at the Throne of Grace in the spirit that our Lord inculcated and in the very words that He dictated.

> In every expression, petition, and argument of this prayer, we *see Jesus:* He and the Father are *one.* He has a "Name" given Him which is above every name. He is the blessed and only Potentate, and His "Kingdom" ruleth over all. He is the "living bread" which came down from Heaven. He had power on earth to "forgive sins." He is able to succour them that are "tempted." He is the Angel that "redeems from all evil." The Kingdom, power, and glory pertain unto Him. He is the fulfilment and confirmation of all Divine promises and gracious assurances. Himself "the Amen, and

faithful Witness." Well did Tertullian term the Lord's Prayer "The Gospel abbreviated." The more clearly we understand the Gospel of the grace of God, "the Gospel of the glory of Christ," the more shall we love this wonderful prayer, and glorying in the Gospel which is "the power of God and the wisdom of God" to them that believe, we shall rejoice with joy unspeakable as we offer the Divinely prescribed petitions and expect gracious answers (Thomas Houston).

1

The Address

"Our Father which art in heaven" (Matt. 6:9).

This opening clause is a suitable preface to all that follows. It presents to us the great *Object* to whom we pray, teaches us the covenant *office* that He sustains to us, and denotes the *obligation* imposed upon us, namely, that of maintaining toward Him a filial spirit, with all that that entails. All real prayer ought to begin with a devout contemplation and to express an acknowledgment of the name of God and of His blessed perfections. We should draw near unto the Throne of Grace with suitable apprehensions of God's sovereign majesty and power, yet with a holy confidence in His fatherly goodness. In these opening words we are plainly instructed to preface our petitions by expressing the sense we have of the essential and relative glories of the One whom we address. The Psalms abound in examples of this. See Psalm 8:1 as a case in point.

"Our Father which art in heaven." Let us first en-

deavor to ascertain the general principle that is em-
bodied in this introductory clause. It informs us in the
simplest possible manner that the great God is most
graciously ready to grant us an audience. By directing us
to address Him as *our Father*, it definitely assures us of
His love and power. This precious title is designed to
raise our affections, to excite us to reverent attention,
and to confirm our confidence in the efficacy of prayer.
Three things are essential to acceptable and effectual
prayer: fervency, reverence, and confidence. This opening clause is designed to stir up each of these essential
elements within us. *Fervency* is the effect of our affections being called into exercise; *reverence* will be promoted by an apprehension of the fact that we are addressing the heavenly throne; *confidence* will be
deepened by viewing the Object of prayer as our Father.

In coming to God in acts of worship, we must "believe
that He is, and that He is a Rewarder of them that diligently seek Him" (Heb. 11:6). What is more calculated
to deepen our confidence and to draw forth the strongest
love and earnest hopes of our hearts toward God, than
Christ's presenting Him to us in His most tender aspect
and endearing relation? How we are here encouraged to
use holy boldness and to pour out our souls before Him!
We could not suitably invoke an impersonal *First Cause;*
still less could we adore or supplicate a great abstraction.
No, it is to a person, a Divine Person, One who has our
best interests at heart, that we are invited to draw near,
even to our *Father*. "Behold, what manner of love the
Father hath bestowed upon us, that *we* should be called
the sons of God" (I John 3:1).

God is the Father of all men *naturally*, being their Creator. "Have we not all one Father? hath not one God created us?" (Mal. 2:10). "But now, O Lord, Thou art our Father; we are the clay, and Thou our Potter; and we all are the work of Thy hand" (Isa. 64:8). The fact that such verses have been grossly perverted by some holding erroneous views on "the universal fatherhood of God and brotherhood of man," must not cause us to utterly repudiate them. It is our privilege to assure the most ungodly and abandoned that, if they will but throw down the weapons of their warfare and do as the prodigal did, there is a loving Father ready to welcome them. If He hears the cries of the ravens (Ps. 147:9), will He turn a deaf ear to the requests of a rational creature? Simon Magus, while still "in the gall of bitterness, and in the bond of iniquity," was directed by an apostle to repent of his wickedness and to *pray* to God (Acts 8:22, 23).

But the depth and full import of this invocation can be entered into only by the believing Christian, for there is a higher relation between him and God than that which is merely of nature. First, God is his Father *spiritually*. Second, God is the Father of His elect because He is the Father of their Lord Jesus Christ (Eph. 1:3). Thus Christ expressly announced, "I ascend unto My Father, and your Father; and to My God, and your God" (John 20:17). Third, God is the Father of His elect by eternal decree: "Having predestinated us unto the *adoption* of children by Jesus Christ to Himself, according to the good pleasure of His will" (Eph. 1:5). Fourth, He is the Father of His elect by *regeneration*, wherein they are born again and become "partakers of the Divine nature"

(II Peter 1:4). It is written, "And because ye are sons, God hath sent forth the Spirit of His Son into your hearts, crying, Abba, Father" (Gal. 4:6).

These words "Our Father" not only signify the office that God sustains to us by virtue of the everlasting covenant, but they also clearly imply our obligation. They teach us both how we ought to dispose ourselves toward God when we pray to Him, and the conduct that is becoming to us by virtue of this relationship. As His children we must "honor" Him (even more than our human parents; see Exod. 20:12; Eph. 6:1–3), be in subjection to Him, delight in Him, and strive in all things to please Him. Again, the phrase "Our Father" not only teaches us our personal interest in God Himself, who by grace is our Father, but it also instructs us of our interest in our fellow Christians, who in Christ are our brethren. It is not merely to "*my* Father" to whom I pray, but to "*our* Father." We must express our love to our brethren by praying for them; we are to be as much concerned about *their* needs as we are over our own. How much is included in these two words!

"Which art in heaven." What a blessed *balance* this gives to the previous phrase. If that tells us of God's goodness and grace, this speaks of His greatness and majesty. If that teaches us of the nearness and dearness of His relationship to us, this announces His infinite elevation above us. If the words "Our Father" inspire confidence and love, then the words "which art in heaven" should fill us with humility and awe. These are the two things that should ever occupy our minds and engage our hearts: the first without the second tends toward unholy familiarity; the second without the first produces coldness and dread. By combining them together, we are preserved from both evils; and a suitable equipoise is wrought and maintained in the soul as we duly contemplate both the mercy and might of God, His unfathomable love and His immeasurable loftiness. Note how the same blessed balance was preserved by the Apostle Paul, when he employed the following words to describe God the Father: "the God of our Lord Jesus Christ, the Father of glory" (Eph. 1:17).

The words "which art in heaven" are *not* used because He is confined there. We are reminded of the words of King Solomon: "But will God indeed dwell on the earth? behold, the heaven and heaven of heavens cannot contain Thee; how much less this house that I have builded?" (I Kings 8:27). God is infinite and omnipresent. There is a particular sense, though, in which the Father *is* "in heaven," for that is the place in which His majesty and glory are most eminently manifested. "Thus saith the Lord, The heaven is *My throne*, and the earth is My footstool" (Isa. 66:1). The realization of this should fill us with the deepest reverence and awe. The words "which art in heaven" call attention to His *providence*, declaring the fact that He is directing all things from on high. These words proclaim His ability to undertake for us, for our Father is *the Almighty*. "But our God is in the heavens: He hath done whatsoever He hath pleased" (Ps. 115:3). Yet though the Almighty, He is "our *Father*." "Like as a father pitieth his children, so the

Lord pitieth them that fear Him" (Ps. 103:13). "If ye then, being evil, know how to give good gifts unto your children: how much more shall your heavenly Father give the Holy Spirit to them that ask Him?" (Luke 11:13). Finally, these blessed words remind us that *we* are journeying *thither,* for heaven is our home.

2

The First Petition

"Hallowed be Thy name" (Matt. 6:9).

"Hallowed be Thy name" is the first of the petitions of Christ's pattern prayer. They are seven in number, and are significantly divided into two groups of three and four respectively: the first three relate to the cause of God; the last four relate to our own daily concerns. A similar division is discernible in the Ten Commandments: the first five teach us our duty toward God (in the fifth, the parents stand to the child in the place of God); the last five teach us our duty toward neighbors. Our primary duty in prayer is to disregard ourselves and to give God the preeminence in our thoughts, desires, and supplications. This petition necessarily comes first, for the glorifying of God's great name is the ultimate end of all things. All other requests must be subordinate to this one and be in pursuance of it. We cannot pray aright unless the glory of God be dominant in our desires. We are to cherish a deep sense of the ineffable holiness of

God and an ardent longing for the honoring of it. Therefore, we must not ask God to bestow anything that would contradict His holiness.

"Hallowed be Thy name." How easy it is to utter these words without any thought of their solemn import! In seeking to ponder them, four questions are naturally raised in our minds. First, what is meant by the word *hallowed?* Second, what is signified by God's *name?* Third, what is the import of "hallowed *be* Thy name?" Fourth, why does this petition come first?

First, the word *hallowed* is a term from Middle English used here to translate a form of the Greek verb *hagiazo.* This term is frequently translated "sanctified." It means "to set apart for a sacred use." Thus, the words "hallowed be Thy name" signify the pious desire that God's matchless name might be reverenced, adored, and glorified, and that God might cause it to be held in the utmost respect and honor, that its fame might spread abroad and be magnified.

Second, the *name* of God stands for *God Himself,* calling to the mind of the believer all that He *is.* We see this in Psalm 5:11: "Let them also that love *Thy name* [that is, *Thyself*] be joyful in Thee." In Psalm 20:1 we read, "The *name* of the God of Jacob defend thee," that is, may the God of Jacob Himself defend thee. "The name of the Lord is a strong tower" (Prov. 18:10), that is to say, Jehovah Himself is a strong tower. The name of God stands for the Divine *perfections.* It is striking to observe that when He "proclaimed the name of the Lord" to Moses, God enumerated His own blessed attributes (see Exod. 34:5-7). This is the true significance of the assertion that "they that know Thy name [that is, Thy wondrous perfections] will put their trust in Thee" (Ps. 9:10). But more particularly, the Divine *name* sets before us all that God has *revealed* to us concerning Himself. It is in such appellations and titles as *the Almighty, the Lord of hosts, Jehovah, the God of peace,* and *our Father* that He has disclosed Himself to us.

Third, what thoughts did the Lord Jesus intend for us to entertain in our hearts when He taught us to pray, "Hallowed be Thy name"? First, in the widest sense, we are to plead thereby that *God,* "by His overruling providence, direct and dispose of all things to His own glory" (*The Westminster Larger Catechism*). Hereby we pray that God Himself sanctify His name—that He cause it, by His providence and grace, to be known and adored through the preaching of His Law and Gospel. Furthermore, we pray that His name might be sanctified and magnified in and by *us.* Not that we can add anything to God's essential holiness, but we can and should promote the manifestative glory of His holiness. That is why we are exhorted thus: "Give unto the Lord the glory due unto His name" (Ps. 96:8). We do not have the power within ourselves to hallow the name of our God. Yet Christ instructs us, by putting an imperative, passive verb in our mouths, to command our Father, saying, "Let Thy name be hallowed!" In this mandatory petition, we are taught to call upon our Father to do what He *must* do, according to the tenor of the words that He spoke through Isaiah: "And concerning the work of My hands *command* ye Me" (Isa. 45:11)! It is because God's name *must* be hallowed among His creatures that our

Master instructs us so to pray. "And this is the confidence that we have in Him, that, if we ask any thing *according to His will*, He heareth us" (I John 5:14). Since our God has so clearly stated His mind, every true believer must desire the hallowing of God's name among men and must be determined to *advance* the revealed glory of God on the earth. We are to do this especially by prayer, since the power to accomplish this great end resides only in God Himself. By prayer we receive the empowering of the Holy Spirit to hallow and glorify God in our own thoughts, words, and deeds.

By praying, "hallowed *be* Thy name," we beg that God, who is most holy and glorious, might enable us to *acknowledge and honor* Him as such. As Manton forcefully expressed it,

> In this petition the glory of God is both desired and promised on our part; for every prayer is both an expression of a desire and also an implicit vow or solemn obligation that we take upon ourselves to prosecute what we ask. Prayer is a preaching to ourselves in God's hearing: we speak to God to warn ourselves—not for His information, but for our edification.

Alas, that this necessary implication of prayer is not more insisted upon in the pulpit today, and more clearly perceived in the pew! We but mock God if we present to Him pious words and have no intention of striving with our might to live in harmony with them.

For us to *hallow* or sanctify His name means that we give God the supreme place, that we set Him above all else in our thoughts, affections, and lives. This high purpose of life is antithetical to the example of the builders of the tower of Babel, who said, "Let us make *us* a name" (Gen. 11:4), and of Nebuchadnezzar, who said, "Is not this great Babylon, that *I* have built for the house of the kingdom by the might of *my* power, and for the honour of *my* majesty?" (Dan. 4:30). The Apostle Peter commands us to "sanctify the Lord God in [our] hearts" (I Peter 3:15). An awe of His majesty and holiness should so fill our hearts that our whole inner beings bow in entire and willing subjection to Him. For this we must pray, striving to obtain right views and a deeper knowledge of Him, that we may worship Him aright and serve Him acceptably.

This petition not only expresses the desire that God sanctify Himself in and through us, enabling us to glorify Him, but it also voices our longing that *others* may know, adore, and glorify Him.

> In the use of this petition we pray that the glory of God may be more and more displayed and advanced in the world in the course of His providence, that His Word may run and be glorified in the conversion and sanctification of sinners, that there may be an increase of holiness in all His people, and that all profanation of the name of God among men may be prevented and removed (John Gill).

Thus, this petition includes the asking of God to grant all needed effusions of the Spirit, to raise up faithful pastors, to move His churches to maintain a Scriptural discipline, and to stir up the saints to an exercise of their graces.

Fourth, it is now obvious why this is the *first* petition in the Lord's Prayer, for it provides the only legitimate basis for all our other requests. The glory of God is to be our chief and great concern. When we offer this petition

to our heavenly Father, we are saying, "Whatever comes
to me, however low I may sink, no matter how deep the
waters be through which I may be called to pass, Lord,
magnify Thyself in and through me." Mark how blessed-
ly this spirit was exemplified by our perfect Savior: "Now
is My soul troubled; and what shall I say? Father, save
Me from this hour: but for this cause came I unto this
hour. Father, glorify *Thy* name" (John 12:27, 28). Though
it was necessary for Him to be baptized with the bap-
tism of suffering, yet the Father's glory was Christ's great
concern.

The following words beautifully summarize the meaning of this petition:

> O Lord, open our eyes that we may know Thee aright and
> may discern Thy power, wisdom, justice, and mercy; and
> enlarge our hearts that we may sanctify Thee in our affec-
> tions, by making Thee our fear, love, joy, and confidence;
> and open our lips that we may bless Thee for Thine infinite
> goodness; yea, O Lord, open our eyes that we may see
> Thee in all Thy works, and incline our wills with reverence
> for Thy name appearing in Thy works, and grant that when
> we use any one of them, that we may honour Thee in our
> sober and sanctified use thereof (W. Perkins).

In conclusion, let us point out very briefly the uses to
be made of this petition. (1) Our past failures are to be
bewailed and confessed. We are to humble ourselves for
those sins whereby we have hindered God's manifestative glory and profaned His name, such as pride of heart,
coldness of zeal, stubbornness of will, and impiety of life.
(2) We are to earnestly seek those graces whereby we
may hallow His name: a fuller knowledge of Himself; an
increase of holy fear in our hearts; increased faith, hope,

love, and worship; and the right use of His gifts. (3) Our duties are to be faithfully practiced, that there may be nothing in our conduct that would cause His name to be blasphemed by unbelievers (Rom. 2:24). "Whether therefore ye eat, or drink, or whatsoever ye do, do all to the glory of God" (I Cor. 10:31).

3

The Second Petition

"Thy Kingdom come" (Matt. 6:10).

The second petition is the most brief and yet the most comprehensive one contained in our Lord's Prayer. Nevertheless, it is strange and sad that, in some circles, it is the least understood and the most controverted. The following questions call for careful consideration. First, what is the *relationship* between this petition and the one preceding it? Second, *whose* Kingdom is here in view? Third, exactly what is meant by the words, "Thy Kingdom"? Fourth, in what sense or senses are we to understand the words, "Thy Kingdom *come*"?

The first petition, "Hallowed be Thy name," concerns God's glory itself, whereas the second and third have respect to the *means* whereby His glory is to be manifested and promoted on earth. God's name is manifestatively glorified here only in the proportion in which His *Kingdom* comes to us and His *will* is done by us. The relationship between this petition and the former one,

then, is quite apparent. Christ teaches us to pray *first* for
the sanctifying of God's great name; then He directs us
to pray subsequently for the means thereto. Among the
means for promoting God's glory, none is so influential
as the coming of His Kingdom. Hence we are exhorted,
"But seek ye first the Kingdom of God and His righteousness" (Matt. 6:33). But though men ought to glorify God's
name upon earth, yet of themselves they cannot do so.
God's Kingdom must first be set up in their hearts. God
cannot be honored by us until we voluntarily submit to
His rule over us.

"Thy Kingdom come." *Whose* Kingdom is being referred to here? Obviously, it is that of God the Father,
yet it is not to be thought of as something separate from
the Kingdom of the Son. The Father's Kingdom is no
more distinct from Christ's than "the Church of the living God" (I Tim. 3:15) is something other than the Body
of Christ, or than the "Gospel of God" (Rom. 1:1) is
something different from "the Gospel of Christ" (Rom.
1:16), or than "the Word of Christ" (Col. 3:16) is to be
distinguished from the Word of God. But Christ *does*
mean, by the words "Thy Kingdom," to distinguish
sharply the Kingdom of God from the kingdom of *Satan*
(Matt. 12:25–28), which is a kingdom of darkness and
disorder. Satan's kingdom is not only opposite in character, but it also stands in belligerent opposition to the
Kingdom of God.

The Father's Kingdom is, first and more generally,
His universal *rule*, His absolute dominion over all creatures and things. "Thine, O Lord, is the greatness, and
the power, and the glory, and the victory, and the

majesty: for all that is in the heaven and in the earth is Thine; Thine is the Kingdom, O Lord, and Thou art exalted as Head above all" (I Chron. 29:11). Second, and more specifically, it is the external sphere of His grace on earth, where He is ostensibly acknowledged (see Matt. 13:11 and Mark 4:11 in their contexts). Third, and more definitely still, it is God's spiritual and internal Kingdom, which is entered by regeneration. "Except a man be born of water and of the Spirit, he cannot enter into the Kingdom of God" (John 3:5).

Now as the Father and the Son are one in nature, so is Their Kingdom the same; and thus it appears in each of its aspects. Concerning the aspect of *providence*, we read, "My Father worketh hitherto, and I work" (John 5:17), signifying cooperation in the government of the world (Heb. 1:3). Christ now holds the *mediatorial* office of a King by virtue of His Father's appointment (Luke 22:29) and establishment (Ps. 2:6). When the Kingdom is viewed very specifically as a *reign of grace* set up in the hearts of God's people, it is rightly called both "the Kingdom of God" (I Cor. 4:20) and "the Kingdom of His dear Son" (Col. 1:13). Viewing the Kingdom in regard to its ultimate eternal *glory*, Christ says that He shall drink the fruit of the vine with us "in [His] Father's Kingdom" (Matt. 26:29), yet it is also called "the everlasting Kingdom of our Lord and Saviour Jesus Christ" (II Peter 1:11). Thus it should seem perfectly natural to us when we read these words: "The kingdoms of this world are become the kingdoms of our Lord, and of His Christ" (Rev. 11:15).

One may ask, "*Which aspect* of the *Kingdom* is here

prayed for as yet future? Certainly not its providential aspect, since *that* has existed and continued from the beginning. The Kingdom must, then, be future in the sense that God's reign of grace is to be consummated in the eternal glory of His Kingdom in the new heavens and new earth (II Peter 3:13). There is to be a voluntary surrender of the whole man—spirit and body—to the revealed will of God, so that His rule over us is entire. But if we are to experience and enjoy the eternal glory of God's Kingdom, we must personally submit to His gracious reign in *this* life. The nature of this reign is summed up in three characteristics: "the Kingdom of God is . . . righteousness, and peace, and joy in the Holy Ghost" (Rom. 14:17). A person experiencing this present reign of grace is characterized by *righteousness* in that the righteousness of Christ is imputed to him as one who, by faith, has become His willing subject; furthermore, he also possesses the righteousness of a good conscience because the Holy Spirit has *sanctified* him, that is, has set him apart to a new life of holiness to the glory of God. Such a person is also characterized by *peace:* peace of conscience toward God, peaceful relations with God's people, and the pursuit of peace with all his fellow creatures (Heb. 12:14). This personal, godly peace is maintained by attention to all the duties of love (Luke 10:27; Rom. 13:8). As the result of righteousness and peace, such a person is also characterized by *joy* in the Holy Spirit, a delighting in God in all the states and vicissitudes of life (Phil. 4:10–14; I Tim. 6:6–10).

There is a threefold application when we pray, "Thy Kingdom *come.*" First, it applies to the external sphere of God's grace here on earth: "Let Thy Gospel be preached and the power of Thy Spirit attend it; let Thy Church be strengthened; let Thy cause on earth be advanced and the works of Satan be destroyed!" Second, it applies to God's internal Kingdom, that is, His spiritual reign of grace within the hearts of men: "Let Thy throne be established in our hearts; let Thy laws be administered in our lives and Thy name be magnified by our walk." Third, it applies to God's Kingdom in its future glory: "Let the Day be hastened when Satan and his hosts shall be completely vanquished, when Thy people shall be done with sinning forever, and when Christ 'shall see of the travail of His soul, and shall be satisfied'" (Isa. 53:11).

God's Kingdom *comes* progressively to individuals in the following degrees or stages: (1) God gives to men the outward means of salvation (Rom. 10:13–17); (2) the preached Word enters the mind, so that the mysteries of the Gospel are understood (Matt. 13:23; Heb. 6:4–6; 10:32); (3) the Holy Spirit regenerates men, so that they enter the Kingdom of God as willing subjects of His gracious reign (John 1:12, 13; 3:3, 5); (4) at death, the spirits of the redeemed are freed from sin (Rom. 7:24, 25; Heb. 12:23); and (5) at the resurrection, the redeemed shall be fully glorified (Rom. 8:23).

> O Lord, let Thy Kingdom come to us who are strangers and pilgrims here on earth: prepare us for it and conduct us into it, that be yet outside of it; renew us by Thy Spirit that we may be subject to Thy will; confirm us who are in the way, that our souls after this life, and both soul and body in the Day of Judgment, may be fully glorified: yea, Lord, hasten this glorification to us and all Thine elect (W. Perkins).

We say again that, though this is the most brief of the petitions, it is also the most comprehensive. In praying, "Thy Kingdom come," we plead for the power and blessing of the Holy Spirit to attend the preaching of the Word, for the Church to be furnished with God-given and God-equipped officers, for the ordinances to be purely administered, for an increase of spiritual gifts and graces in Christ's members, and for the overthrow of Christ's enemies. Thus we pray that the Kingdom of grace may be further extended till the whole of God's elect are brought into it. Also, by necessary implication, we pray that God will wean us more and more from the perishing things of this world.

In conclusion, let us point out some of the *uses* to which this petition should be put. First, we ought to bewail and confess our own *failures* to promote the Kingdom of God, and those of others. It is our duty to confess before God our wretched, natural depravity and the awful proclivity of our flesh to serve sin and the interests of Satan (Rom. 7:14–24). We ought to mourn the sad state of the world and its woeful transgressions of God's Law, by which God is dishonored and the kingdom of Satan furthered (Ps. 119:136; Mark 3:5). Second, we are to earnestly seek those *graces* that will make our lives a sanctifying influence in the world, in order that God's Kingdom might be both built and maintained. We are to endeavor to so subject ourselves to the commandments of Christ that we are wholly ruled by Him, always ready to do His bidding (Rom. 6:13). Third, having prayed for God's enabling, we are to perform all the duties appointed to us by God, bringing forth the fruits that pertain to God's Kingdom (Matt. 21:43; Rom. 14:17). This we are to do with all diligence (Eccles. 9:10; Col. 3:17), using all the Divinely appointed means for the furthering of God's Kingdom.

This second petition is well summarized in *The Westminster Shorter Catechism:*

> In the second petition... we pray, that Satan's kingdom may be destroyed; and that the Kingdom of grace may be advanced, ourselves and others brought into it, and kept in it; and that the Kingdom of glory may be hastened.

4

The Third Petition

"Thy will be done in earth, as it is in heaven" (Matt. 6:10).

The connection between this third petition and the preceding ones is not difficult to trace. The first concern of our hearts, as well as our prayers, must be for God's glory. Longings after God's Kingdom naturally follow, as do honest endeavors to serve Him while we remain on this earth. The glory of God is the great object of our *desires*. The coming and enlargement of His Kingdom are the chief *means* by which God's glory is manifestatively secured. Our personal obedience makes it *manifest* that His Kingdom *has* come to us. When God's Kingdom really comes to one's soul, he must, of necessity, be brought into obedience to its laws and ordinances. It is worse than useless to call God our King if His commandments are disregarded by us. Broadly speaking, there are two parts to this petition: (1) a request for the spirit of obedience; and (2) a statement of the manner in which obedience is to be rendered.

"Thy will be done." This clause may present a difficulty to a few of our readers, who may ask, "Is not God's
will always done?" In one respect it is, but in another
respect it is not. Scripture presents the will of God from
two distinct viewpoints: His secret will and His revealed
will, or His decretive and His preceptive will. His secret
or decretive will is the rule of *His own* actions: in creation (Rev. 4:11), in providence (Dan. 4:35), and in grace
(Rom. 9:15). That which God has decreed is always unknown to men until revealed by prophecies of things to
come or by events as they transpire. On the other hand,
God's revealed or preceptive will is the rule for our actions, God having made known in the Scriptures that
which is pleasing in His sight.

The secret or decretive will of God is always done,
equally on earth as in heaven, for none can thwart or
even hinder it. It is equally evident that God's revealed
will is violated every time one of His precepts is disobeyed. This distinction was clearly drawn when Moses
said to Israel, "The *secret* things belong unto the Lord
our God; but those things which are *revealed* belong
unto us and to our children for ever, that we may *do* all
the words of this Law" (Deut. 29:29). This distinction is
also found in the use of the word *counsel.* "My counsel
[God's eternal *decree*] *shall* stand, and I *will* do *all* My
pleasure" (Isa. 46:10), says Jehovah. But in Luke 7:30 we
read that "the Pharisees and lawyers *rejected* [that is,
frustrated] the counsel [or revealed will] of God" as to
themselves, being not baptized by John. On the one
hand we read, "For who hath resisted His will?" (Rom.
9:19). On the other hand we are told, "For this is the will

of God, even your sanctification" (I Thess. 4:3). The revealed or preceptive will of God is stated in God's Word, defining our duty and making known the path in which we should walk. God has provided His Word as the appointed means for the renewing of our minds. A laying up of God's precepts in the heart (Ps. 119:11) is essential to the transforming of one's character and conduct; this vital discipline is an absolute prerequisite to our proving, in our own Christian experience, "what is that good, and acceptable, and perfect, will of God" (Rom. 12:2).

The will of God, then, is a phrase that, taken by itself, may express either what God has purposed to do or what He has commanded to be done by us. With regard to the will of God in the first sense, it always is, always has been, and ever shall be done upon earth as it is in heaven, for neither human policy nor infernal power can prevent it. The text now before us contains a prayer that we might be brought into complete accord with God's *revealed* will. We *do* the will of God when, out of a due regard for His authority, we regulate our own thoughts and conduct by His commandments. Such is our bounden duty, and it should ever be our fervent desire and diligent endeavor so to do. We mock God if we present this request and then fail to make the conforming of ourselves to His revealed will our main business. Ponder our Lord's solemn warning in Matthew 15:1–9 (cf. Matt. 25:31–46 and Luke 6:46–49).

"Thy will be done in earth." The one who sincerely prays this necessarily intimates his unreserved surrender to God; he implies his renunciation of the will of Satan (II Tim. 2:26) and of his own corrupt inclinations (I Peter

4:2), and his rejection of all things opposed to God. Nevertheless, such a soul is painfully conscious that there is still much in him that is in conflict with God. He therefore humbly and contritely acknowledges that he cannot do His Father's will without Divine assistance, and that he earnestly desires and seeks enabling grace. Possibly the meaning and scope of this petition will best be opened up if we express it thus: O Father, let Thy will be revealed *to* me, let it be wrought *in* me, and let it be performed *by* me.

From a positive perspective, when we pray, "Thy will be done," we beg God for spiritual *wisdom* to learn His will: "Make me to understand the way of Thy precepts.... Teach me, O Lord, the way of Thy statutes" (Ps. 119:27, 33). Also, we beg God for spiritual *inclination* toward His will: "I will run the way of Thy commandments, when Thou shalt enlarge my heart.... Incline my heart unto Thy testimonies" (Ps. 119:32, 36). Furthermore, we beg God for spiritual *strength* to perform His bidding: "Quicken Thou me according to Thy Word.... strengthen Thou me according unto Thy Word" (Ps. 119:25, 28; cf. Phil. 2:12, 13; Heb. 13:20, 21). Our Lord teaches us to pray, "Thy will be done *in earth*," because this is the place of our discipleship. This is the realm in which we are to practice self-denial. If we do not do His will here, we never shall in heaven.

"As it is in heaven." The standard by which we are to measure our attempts at doing God's will on earth is nothing less than the conduct of the saints and angels in heaven. *How* is God's will done in heaven? Certainly it is not done reluctantly or sullenly, nor is it done hypocritically or Pharisaically. We may be sure that it is executed neither tardily nor fitfully, neither partially nor fragmentarily. In the heavenly courts, God's will is performed gladly and joyfully. Both the four living creatures (not *beasts*) and the twenty-four elders in Revelation 5:8–14 are depicted as rendering worship and service together. Yet heavenly adoration and obedience are rendered humbly and reverently, for the seraphim veil their faces before the Lord (Isa. 6:2). There God's commands are executed with alacrity, for Isaiah says that one of the seraphim *flew* to him from the Divine presence (Isa. 6:6). There God is lauded constantly and untiringly. "Therefore are [the saints] before the throne of God, and serve Him *day and night* in His temple" (Rev. 7:15). The angels obey God promptly, wholly, perfectly, and with ineffable delight. But *we* are sinful and full of infirmities. With what propriety, then, can the obedience of celestial beings be proposed as a present example for us? We raise this question not as a concession to our imperfections, but because honest souls are exercised by it.

First, this standard is set before us *to sweeten* our subjection to the Divine will, for we on earth are set no more demanding task than are those in heaven. Heaven is what it is because the will of God is done by all who dwell there. The measure in which a foretaste of its bliss may be obtained by us upon earth will be determined largely by the degree to which we perform here the Divine bidding. Second, this standard is given to show us the blessed *reasonableness* of our obedience to God. "Bless the Lord, ye His angels, that excel in strength, that do His commandments, hearkening unto the voice of His Word" (Ps. 103:20). Then can God require less of us? If we are to have communion with the angels in glory, then we must be conformed to them in grace. Third, it is given as the standard at which we must ever aim. Paul says, "For this cause we . . . do not cease to pray for you . . . That ye might walk worthy of the Lord unto all pleasing. . . . that ye may stand perfect and complete in all the will of God" (Col. 1:9, 10; 4:12). Fourth, this standard is given to teach us not only *what* to do, but *how* to do it. We are to imitate the angels in the *manner* of their obedience, though we cannot equal them in measure or degree.

"Thy will be done in earth, as it is in heaven." Weigh this attentively in the light of what precedes. First, we are taught to pray, *"Our Father* which art in heaven"; then should we not do His will? We must, if we are His children, for disobedience is that which characterizes His enemies. Did not His own dear Son render Him perfect obedience? And it should delight us to strive to render Him the quality of devotion to which He is accustomed in the place of His peculiar abode, the seat of our future bliss. Second, since we are taught to pray, *"Hallowed be thy name,"* does not a real concern for God's glory oblige us to make a conformity to His will our supreme quest? We certainly must if we desire to honor God, for nothing dishonors Him more than self-will and defiance. Third, since we are instructed to pray, *"Thy Kingdom come,"* should we not seek to be in full subjection to its laws and ordinances? We must, if we are subjects thereof, for it is only alienated rebels who despise His scepter.

5

The Fourth Petition

"Give us this day our daily bread" (Matt. 6:11).

We turn our attention to those petitions that more immediately concern ourselves. The fact that our Lord placed three petitions that relate directly to God's legitimate interests *first* should sufficiently indicate to us that we must labor in prayer to promote the manifestative glory of God, to advance His Kingdom, and to do His will before we are permitted to supplicate for our *own* needs. These petitions that more immediately concern ourselves are four in number, and in them we may clearly discern an implied reference to each of the Persons of the blessed Trinity. Our temporal needs are supplied by the kindness of the Father. Our sins are forgiven through the mediation of the Son. We are preserved from temptation and delivered from evil by the gracious operations of the Holy Spirit. Let us carefully note the *proportion* that is observed in these last four petitions: one of them concerns our bodily needs; three relate to the concerns of the soul. This teaches us that in prayer, as in all other activities of life, temporal concerns are to be subordinated to spiritual concerns.

"Give us this day our daily bread." Perhaps it will be helpful if we begin by raising a number of questions. First, why does this request for the supply of bodily needs come *before* those petitions that concern the needs of the soul? Second, what is signified by, and included in, the term *bread?* Third, in what sense may we suitably beg God for our daily bread when we already have a supply on hand? Fourth, how can bread be a Divine gift if we earn the same by our own labors? Fifth, what is our Lord inculcating by restricting the request to "our daily bread"? Before attempting to answer these queries let us say that, with almost all of the best of the commentators, we regard the prime reference as being to *material* bread rather than to spiritual.

Matthew Henry has astutely pointed out that the reason this request for the supply of our physical needs *heads* the last four petitions is that "our natural [well-being] is necessary [for] our spiritual well-being in this world." In other words, God grants to us the physical things of this life as *helps* to the discharge of our spiritual duties. And since they are given by Him, they are to be employed in His service. What gracious consideration God shows toward our weakness: we are unapt and unfit to perform our higher duties if deprived of the things needed for the sustenance of our bodily existence. We may also rightly infer that this petition comes first in order to promote the steady growth and strengthening of our faith. Perceiving the goodness and faithfulness of

God in supplying our daily physical needs, we are encouraged and stimulated to ask for higher blessings (cf. Acts 17:25–28).

"Our daily bread" refers primarily to the supply of our temporal needs. With the Hebrews, *bread* was a generic term, signifying the necessities and conveniences of this life (Gen. 3:19; 28:20), such as food, raiment, and housing. Inherent in the use of the specific term *bread* rather than the more general term *food* is an emphasis teaching us to ask not for dainties or for riches, but for that which is wholesome and needful. *Bread* here includes health and appetite, apart from which food does us no good. It also takes into account our *nourishment:* for this comes not from the food alone, nor does it lie within the power of man's will. Hence God's *blessing* on it is to be sought. "For every creature of God is good, and nothing to be refused, if it be received with thanksgiving: For it is sanctified by the Word of God and prayer" (I Tim. 4:4, 5).

In begging God to give us our daily bread, we ask that He might graciously provide us with a portion of outward things such as He sees will be best suited to our calling and station. "Give me neither poverty nor riches; feed me with food convenient for me: Lest I be full, and deny Thee, and say, Who is the Lord? or lest I be poor, and steal, and take the name of my God in vain" (Prov. 30:8, 9). If God grants us the superfluities of life, we are to be thankful, and must endeavor to use them to His glory; but we must not ask for them. "And having food and raiment let us be therewith *content*" (I Tim. 6:8). We are to ask for "*our* daily bread." It is to be obtained not by

theft, nor by taking by force or fraud what belongs to
another, but by our personal labor and industry. "Love
not sleep, lest thou come to poverty; open thine eyes,
and thou shalt be satisfied with bread" (Prov. 20:13).
"She looketh well to the ways of her household, and
eateth not the bread of idleness" (Prov. 31:27).

How can I sincerely ask God for this day's bread when
I already have a good supply on hand? First, I may ask
this because my present temporal portion may speedily
be taken from me, and that without any warning. A striking and solemn illustration of this is found in Genesis
19:15–25. Fire may burn down one's house and everything in it. So by asking God for the daily supply of our
temporal needs, we acknowledge our complete depen-
dency upon His bounty. Second, we should plead this
petition every day, because what we have will profit us
nothing unless God deigns also to *bless* the same to us.
Third, love requires that I pray this way, because this
petition comprehends far more than my own personal
needs. By teaching us to pray, "Give *us* this day *our*
daily bread," the Lord Jesus is inculcating love and compassion toward others. God requires us to love our
neighbor as ourselves, and to be as solicitous about the
needs of our fellow Christians as we are of our own needs
(Gal. 6:10).

How can God be said to *give* us our daily bread if we
ourselves have earned it? Surely such a quibble scarcely
needs reply. First, God must give it to us because our
right to it was forfeited when we fell in Adam. Second,
God must bestow it because everything belongs to Him.
"The earth is the *Lord's*, and the fulness thereof; the

world, and they that dwell therein" (Ps. 24:1). "The silver is Mine, and the gold is Mine, saith the Lord of hosts" (Hag. 2:8). "Therefore will I return, and take away *My* corn in the time thereof, and *My* wine in the season thereof" (Hos. 2:9). Therefore we hold in fee from our Lord (that is, on condition of homage and service) the portion He bestows. We are but *stewards*. God grants us both possession and use of His creation, but retains to Himself the title. Third, we ought to pray this way because all that we have comes *from God*. "These wait all upon Thee; that Thou mayest give them their meat in due season. That Thou givest them they gather: Thou openest Thine hand, they are filled with good" (Ps. 104:27, 28; cf. Acts 14:17). Although by labor and purchase things may be said to be *ours* (relatively speaking), yet it is God who gives us strength *to labor*.

What is Christ inculcating by restricting the request to "our *daily* bread"? First, we are reminded of our *frailty*. We are unable to continue in health for twenty-four hours, and are unfit for the duties of a single day, unless constantly fed from on high. Second, we are reminded of the *brevity* of our mundane existence. None of us knows what a day may bring forth, and therefore we are forbidden to boast ourselves of tomorrow (Prov. 27:1). Third, we are taught to suppress all anxious concern for the future and to live a day at a time. "Take therefore no thought for the morrow: for the morrow shall take thought for the things of itself. Sufficient unto the day is the evil thereof" (Matt. 6:34). Fourth, Christ inculcates the lesson of *moderation*. We are to stifle the spirit of covetousness by forming the habit of being contented with a slender portion. Finally, observe that our Lord's words, "Give us *this* day our daily bread," are appropriate for use each morning, whereas the expression He teaches in Luke 11:3, "Give us *day by day* our daily bread," ought to be our request every night.

In summary, then, this petition teaches us the following indispensable lessons: (1) that it is permissible and lawful to supplicate God for temporal mercies; (2) that we are completely dependent upon God's bounty for everything; (3) that our confidence is to be in Him alone, and not in secondary causes; (4) that we should be grateful, and return thanks for material blessings as well as for spiritual ones; (5) that we should practice frugality and discourage covetousness; (6) that we should have family worship every morning and evening; and (7) that we should be equally solicitous on behalf of others as for ourselves.

6

The Fifth Petition

"And forgive us our debts, as we forgive our debtors"
(Matt. 6:12).

At the outset of our consideration of this fifth petition, it is vital that we give due attention to the fact that it *begins* differently than the first four. For the first time in our Lord's Prayer we encounter the word *and*. The fourth petition, "Give us this day our daily bread," is followed by the words, "*And* forgive us our debts," indicating that there is a very close connection between the two petitions. It is true that the first three petitions are intimately related, yet they are quite distinct. But the fourth and fifth petitions are to be especially linked in our minds for several practical reasons. First, we are taught that without pardon all the good things of this life will benefit us nothing. A man in a cell on death row is fed and clothed, but what is the daintiest diet and the costliest apparel worth to him as long as he remains under sentence of imminent death? "Our daily bread doth but fatten us as lambs for the slaughter if our sins be not pardoned" (Matthew Henry). Second, our Lord would inform us that our sins are so many and so grievous that we deserve not one mouthful of food. Each day the Christian is guilty of offenses that forfeit even the common blessings of life, so that he should ever say with Jacob, "I am not worthy of the least of all the mercies... which Thou hast shewed unto Thy servant" (Gen. 32:10). Third, Christ would remind us that our sins are the great obstacle to the favors we might receive from God (Isa. 59:2; Jer. 5:25). Our sins constrict the channel of blessing, and therefore as often as we pray, "Give us," we must add, "And forgive us." Fourth, Christ would encourage us to go on in faith from strength to strength. If we trust God's providence to provide for our bodies, should we not trust Him for the salvation of our souls from the power and dominion of sin and from sin's dreadful wages?

"Forgive us our debts." Our sins are here viewed, as in Luke 11:4, under the notion of *debts*, that is, undischarged obligations or failures to render to God His lawful due. We owe to God sincere and perfect worship together with earnest and perpetual obedience. The Apostle Paul says, "Therefore, brethren, we are debtors, not to the flesh, to live after the flesh" (Rom. 8:12), thus stating the negative side. But positively, we are debtors *to God*, to live unto Him. By the law of creation, we were made not to gratify the flesh but to glorify God. "When ye shall have done all those things which are commanded you, say, We are unprofitable servants: we have done that which was *our duty* to do" (Luke 17:10). Failure to discharge our debt of worship and obedience has entailed guilt, bringing us into debt to Divine justice. Now when we pray, "Forgive us our *debts,*" we do not ask to be discharged from the duties we owe to God, but to be acquitted from our guilt, that is, to have the punishment due us remitted.

"There was a certain creditor which had two debtors" (Luke 7:41). Here, in our text, God is set forth under the figure of *a creditor,* partly in view of His being our Creator, and partly as being our Lawgiver and Judge. God not only has endowed us with talents, obligating us to serve and glorify our Benefactor, but also has placed us under His Law, so that we are condemned for our defaults. And as Judge, He will yet call upon each of us to render a full account of our respective stewardships (Rom. 14:12). There is to be a great Day of Reckoning (Luke 19:15), and those who have *failed* to repent of and bewail their debts and to take refuge in Christ will be eternally punished for their defaults. Alas, that so very few conduct themselves in the conscious realization of that solemn Assize.

Not only does this metaphor of creditor and debtors apply to our ruin, but, thank God, it applies equally to the *remedy* for our recovery. As insolvent debtors, we are completely undone and must forever lie under the righteous judgment of God, unless full compensation be made to Him. But *we* are powerless to pay Him that compensation, for, morally and spiritually speaking, we are undischarged bankrupts. Deliverance, then, must come from outside ourselves. Here is where the Gospel speaks relief to the sin-burdened soul: another, even the Lord Jesus, took upon Himself the office of Sponsor, and rendered full satisfaction to Divine justice on behalf of His people, making complete compensation to God for

them. Hence, in this connection, Christ is called the
"Surety of a better testament" (Heb. 7:22), as He af-
firmed prophetically through His father David: "Then I
restored that which I took not away" (Ps. 69:4). God declares concerning His elect, "Deliver him from going
down to the pit: I have a found *a ransom*" (Job 33:24).

"And forgive us our debts." Strange to say, some experience a difficulty here. Seeing that God has already
forgiven the Christian "all trespasses" (Col. 2:13), is it
not needless, they ask, for him to continue *to beg* God
for forgiveness? This difficulty is self-created, through a
failure to distinguish between the purchase of our pardon by Christ and its actual application to us. True, full
atonement for all our sins was made by Him, and at the
cross their guilt was canceled. True, all our *old sins* are
purged at our conversion (II Peter 1:9). Nevertheless,
there is a very real sense in which our present and future
sins are *not* remitted until we repent and confess them
to God. Therefore, it is both necessary and proper that
we should seek pardon for them. (I John 1:6–10). Even
after Nathan administered assurance to David, saying,
"The Lord also hath put away thy sins" (II Sam. 12:13),
David begged God's forgiveness (Ps. 51:1).

What do we ask for in this petition? First, we ask that
God will not lay to our charge the sins we daily commit
(Ps. 143:2). Second, we plead that God will accept the
satisfaction of Christ for our sins and look upon us as
righteous in Him. Some may object, "But if we be real
Christians, He has *already* done so." True, yet He re-
quires us to sue for our pardon, just as He said to Christ,
"*Ask* of Me, and I shall give Thee the heathen for Thine

inheritance" (Ps. 2:8). God is ready to forgive, but He requires us to call upon Him. Why? That His saving mercy may be acknowledged, and that our faith may be exercised! Third, we beseech God for the *continuance* of pardon. Though we be justified, yet we must continue to ask; as with our daily bread, though we have a goodly store on hand, yet we beg for the continuance of it. Fourth, we plead for the *sense* of forgiveness or assurance of it, that sins may be blotted out of our conscience and from God's book of remembrance. The effects of forgiveness are inner peace and access to God (Rom. 5:1,2).

Forgiveness is not to be demanded as something due us, but requested as a mercy. "To the very end of life, the best Christian must come for forgiveness just as he did at first, not as a claimant of a right but as a suppliant of a favour" (John Brown). Nor is this anywise inconsistent with, or a reflection upon, our complete justification (Acts 13:39). It is certain that the believer "shall not come into condemnation" (John 5:24); yet instead of this truth leading him to the conclusion that he need not pray for the remission of his sins, it supplies him with the strongest possible encouragement to present such a petition. Likewise, the Divine assurance that a genuine Christian shall persevere to the end, instead of laying a foundation for carelessness, is a most powerful motive to watchfulness and faithfulness. This petition implies a felt sense of sin, a penitent acknowledgement thereof, a seeking of God's mercy for Christ's sake, and the realization that He can righteously pardon us. Its presentation should ever be preceded by self-examination and humiliation.

Our Lord teaches us to confirm this petition with *an argument:* "as we forgive our debtors." First, Christ teaches us to argue from a like disposition in ourselves: whatever good there be in us must first be in God, for He is the sum of all excellency; if, then, a kindly disposition has been planted in our hearts by His Holy Spirit, the same must be found in Him. Second, we are to reason with God from the lesser to the greater: if we, who have but a drop of mercy, can forgive the offenses done to us, surely God, who is a veritable Ocean of mercy, will forgive us. Third, we are to argue from the condition of those who may expect pardon: we are sinners who, out of a sense of God's mercy to us, are disposed to show mercy to others; hence, we are morally qualified for more mercy, seeing that we have not abused the mercy we have already received. They who would rightly pray to God for pardon must pardon those who wrong them. Joseph (Gen. 50:14–21) and Stephen (Acts 7:60) are conspicuous examples. We need to pray much for God to remove all bitterness and malice from our hearts against those who wrong us. But to forgive our debtors does not exclude our rebuking them, and, where public interests are involved, having them prosecuted. It would be my duty to hand over a burglar to a policeman, or to go to law against one who was able but who refused to pay me (Rom. 13:1–8). If a fellow citizen is guilty of a crime and I do not report it, then I become an accessory to that crime. I thus betray a lack of love for him and for society (Lev. 19:17, 18).

7

The Sixth Petition

"And lead us not into temptation" (Matt. 6:13).

This sixth petition also begins with the word *and*, requiring us to mark closely its relationship with the preceding petition. The connection between them may be set forth thus. First, the previous petition concerns the negative side of our justification, while this one has to do with our practical sanctification; for the two blessings must never be severed. Thus we see that the *balance* of truth is again perfectly preserved. Second, past sins being pardoned, we should pray fervently for grace to prevent us from repeating them. We cannot rightly desire God to forgive us our sins unless we sincerely long for grace to abstain from the like in the future. We should therefore make it our practice to beg earnestly for strength to avoid a repetition of them. Third, in the fifth petition we pray for the remission of the guilt of sin; here we ask for deliverance from its power. God's granting of the former request is to encourage faith in us to ask Him to mortify the flesh and to vivify the spirit.

Before proceeding further, it may be best to clear the
way by disposing of something that is a real difficulty to
many. "Let no man say when he is tempted, I am tempted of God: for God cannot be tempted with evil, neither
tempteth He any man" (James 1:13). There is no more
conflict between the words "And lead us not into temptation" and the expression "neither tempteth He any man"
than there is the slightest opposition between the teaching that "God cannot be tempted with evil" and the
recorded fact that Israel "turned back and tempted God"
(Ps. 78:41). That God tempts no man means that He
neither infuses evil into anyone nor is in any wise a
partner with us in our guilt. The criminality of our sins is
to be wholly attributed to ourselves, as James 1:14, 15,
makes clear. But men *deny* that it is from their own
corrupt natures that such and such evils proceed, blam-
ing their temptations. And if they are unable to fix the
evil on those temptations, then they seek to excuse
themselves by throwing the blame upon God, as Adam
did: "The woman whom *Thou* gavest to be with me, she
gave me of the tree, and I did eat" (Gen. 3:12).

It is important to understand that the word *tempt* has
a twofold significance in Scripture, though it is not always easy to determine which of the two applies in a
particular passage: (1) *to try (the strength of), to put to
the test;* and (2) *to entice to do evil.* When it is said that
"God did tempt Abraham" (Gen. 22:1), it means that He
tried him, putting to the test his faith and fidelity. But
when we read that Satan tempted Christ, it signifies that
Satan sought to bring about His downfall, morally impos-
sible though it was. To *tempt* is to make trial of a person,

in order to find out what he is and what he will do. We may tempt God in a legitimate and good way by putting Him to the test in a way of *duty*, as when we await the fulfillment of His promise in Malachi 3:10. But, as is recorded for our admonition in Psalm 78:41, Israel tempted God in a way of *sin*, acting in such a manner as to provoke His displeasure.

"And lead us not into temptation." Note the truths that are clearly *implied* by these words. First, God's universal providence is owned. All creatures are at the sovereign disposal of their Maker; He has the same absolute control over evil as over good. In this petition an acknowledgment is made that the *ordering* of all temptations is in the hands of our all-wise, omnipotent God. Second, God's offended justice and the evil we deserve are avowed. Our wickedness is such that God would be perfectly just if He should now allow us to be completely swallowed up by sin and destroyed by Satan. Third, His mercy is recognized. Though we have so grievously provoked Him, yet for Christ's sake He has remitted our debts. Therefore, we plead that He will henceforth preserve us. Fourth, our weakness is acknowledged. Because we realize that we are unable to stand against temptations in our own strength, we pray, "And lead us not into temptation."

How does God lead us into temptation? First, He does so *objectively* when His providences, though good in themselves, offer occasions (because of our depravity) for sin. When we manifest self-righteousness, He may lead us into circumstances something like Job experienced. When we are self-confident, He may be pleased to suffer us to be tempted as Peter was. When we are self-complacent, He may bring us into a situation similar to the one Hezekiah encountered (II Chron. 32:27–31; cf. II Kings 20:12–19). God leads many into poverty, which though a sore trial is yet, under His blessing, often enriching to the soul. God leads some into prosperity, which is a great snare to many. Yet if sanctified by Him, prosperity enlarges one's capacity for usefulness. Second, God tempts *permissively* when He does not restrain Satan (which He is under no obligation to do). Sometimes God suffers him to sift us as wheat, just as a strong wind snaps off dead boughs from living trees. Third, God tempts some men *judicially*, punishing their sins by allowing the Devil to lead them into further sin, to the ultimate destruction of their souls.

But *why* does God tempt His people, either objectively by His providences, or subjectively and permissively by Satan? He does so for various reasons. First, He tries us in order to reveal to us our weakness and our deep need of His grace. God withdrew His sustaining arm from Hezekiah in order "that he might know all that was in his heart" (II Chron. 32:31). When God leaves us to ourselves, it is a most painful and humiliating discovery that we make. Yet it is needful if we are to pray from the heart, "Hold *Thou* me up, and I shall be safe" (Ps. 119:117). Second, He tests us in order to teach us the need of watchfulness and prayer. Most of us are so stupid and unbelieving that we learn only in the hard school of experience, and even its lessons have to be *knocked* into us. Little by little we discover how dearly we have to pay for rashness, carelessness, and presumption. Third, our

Father subjects us to trials in order to cure our slothfulness. God calls out, "Awake thou that sleepest" (Eph. 5:14), but we heed Him not; and therefore He often employs rough servants to rudely arouse us. Fourth, God puts us to the test in order to reveal to us the importance and value of the armor He has appointed (Eph. 6:11–18). If we *heedlessly* go forth to battle without our spiritual panoply, then we must not be surprised at the wounds we receive; but they shall have the salutary effect of making us more careful for the future!

From all that has been said above, it should be clear that we are not to pray simply and absolutely against all temptations. Christ Himself was tempted by the Devil, and was definitely led into the wilderness by the Spirit for that very end (Matt. 4:1; Mark 1:12). Not all temptations are evil, regardless of the aspect in which we view them: their nature, their design, or their outcome. It is from the *evil* of temptations that we pray to be spared (as the next petition in the prayer indicates), yet even in that we pray submissively and with qualification. We are to pray that we may not be led into temptation; or, if God sees fit that we should be tempted, that we may not yield thereto; or if we yield, that we be not totally overcome by the sin. Nor may we pray for a total exemption from trials, but only for a removal of the *judgment* of them. God often permits Satan to assault and harass us, in order to humble us, to drive us to Himself, and to glorify Himself by manifesting more fully to us His preserving power. "My brethren, count it all joy when ye fall into divers temptations; Knowing this, that the trying of your faith worketh patience" (James 1:2, 3).

In conclusion, a few remarks upon *our responsibility* in connection with temptation are appropriate. First, it is our bounden duty to avoid those persons and places that would allure us into sin, just as it is always our duty to be on the alert for the first signs of Satan's approach (Ps. 19:13; Prov. 4:14; I Thess. 5:22). As an unknown writer has said, "He who carries about with him so much inflammable material would do well to keep the greatest possible distance from the fire." Second, we must steadfastly resist the Devil. "Take us the foxes, the *little* foxes, that spoil the vines" (Song of Sol. 2:15). We must not yield a single inch to our enemy. Third, we are to go to God for grace submissively, for the measure He grants us is according to His own good pleasure (Phil. 2:13).

> You are to endeavour, indeed, to pray, and use all good means to come out of temptation; but submit, if the Lord be pleased to continue His exercise upon you. Nay, though God should continue the temptation, and for the present not give out those measures of grace necessary for you, yet you must not murmur, but lie at His feet; for God is Lord of His own grace (Thomas Manton).

Thus we learn that this petition is to be presented in subservience to God's sovereign will.

8

The Seventh Petition

"But deliver us from evil" (Matt. 6:13).

This seventh petition brings us to the end of the petitionary part of our Lord's Prayer. The four requests that are for the supply of our own needs are for *providing* grace ("give us"), *pardoning* grace ("forgive us"), *preventing* grace ("lead us not into temptation"), and *preserving* grace ("deliver us"). It is to be carefully noted that in each case the pronoun is in the plural number and not the singular—*us* and *our*, not *me* and *my*. For we are to supplicate not for ourselves only, but for all the members of the household of faith (Gal. 6:10). How beautifully this demonstrates the *family* character of truly Christian prayer. For our Lord teaches us to address "our Father" and to embrace all His children in our requests. On the high priest's breastplate were inscribed the names of all the tribes of Israel—a symbol of Christ's intercession on high. So, too, the Apostle Paul enjoins "supplication for *all* saints" (Eph. 6:18). Self-love shuts up the bowels of compassion, confining us to our own interests; but the love of God shed abroad in our hearts makes us solicitous on behalf of our brethren.

"But deliver us from evil." We cannot agree with those who restrict the application of the word *evil* here to the Devil alone, though doubtless he is principally intended. The Greek may, with equal propriety, be rendered either *the evil one* or *the evil thing;* in fact, it is translated both ways.

> We are taught to pray for deliverance from all kinds, degrees, and occasions of evil; from the malice, power, and subtlety of the powers of darkness; from this evil world and all its allurements, snares, tempers, and deceits; from the evil of our own hearts, that it may be restrained, subdued, and finally extirpated; and from the evil of suffering... (Thomas Scott).

This petition, then, expresses a desire to be delivered from all that is really prejudicial to us, and especially from sin, which has no good in it.

It is true that in contradistinction to God, who is the Holy One, Satan is designated "the wicked [or evil] one" (Eph. 6:16; I John 2:13, 14; 3:12; 5:18, 19). Yet it is also true that sin is evil (Rom. 12:9), the world is evil (Gal. 1:4), and our own corrupt nature is evil (Matt. 12:35). Moreover, the advantages that the Devil gains over us are by means of the flesh and the world, for *they* are his agents. Thus, this is a prayer for deliverance from all our spiritual enemies. It is true that we *have been* delivered from "the power of darkness" and translated into the Kingdom of Christ (Col. 1:13), and that, as a consequence, Satan no longer has any *lawful* authority over us. Nevertheless, our adversary wields an awesome and oppressive power: though he cannot rule us, he is permitted to molest and harass us. He stirs up enemies to persecute us (Rev. 12, 13), he inflames our lusts (I Chron. 21:1; I Cor. 7:5), and he disturbs our peace (I Peter 5:8). It is therefore our constant need and duty to pray for deliverance from him.

Satan's favorite device is to incite or to deceive us into a prolonged self-indulgence in some one sin to which we are particularly inclined. Therefore, we need to be in constant prayer that our natural corruptions may be mortified. When he cannot cause some gross lust to tyrannize a child of God, he labors to get him to commit some evil deed whereby the name of God will be dishonored and His people offended, as he did in the case of David (II Sam. 11). When a believer has fallen into sin the Devil seeks to make him easy therein, so that he has no remorse for it. When God chastens us for our faults, Satan strives to make us fret against our Father's chastening or else to drive us to despair. When he fails in these methods of attack, then he stirs up our friends and relatives to oppose us, as in the case of Job. But whatever be his line of assault, prayer for deliverance must be our daily recourse.

Christ Himself has left us an example that should encourage us to offer this petition, for in His intercession on our behalf we find Him saying, "I pray not that Thou shouldest take them out of the world, but that Thou shouldest keep them from the evil" (John 17:15). Observe how this explains to us the *connection* between the clause we are now considering and the one that precedes it. Christ did not pray absolutely that we should be exempted from temptation, for He knew that His people must expect assaults both from within and from without. Therefore, He asked not that we should be taken out of this world, but that we be delivered from the evil. To be kept from the evil of sin is a far greater mercy than to be kept from the trouble of temptation. But how far, it may be asked, has God undertaken to deliver us from evil? First, He keeps us from evil so far as it would be hurtful to our highest interests. It was for Peter's ultimate good, and the good of God's people, that he was suffered to fall temporarily (Luke 22:31–34). Second, God prevents evil from gaining full dominion over us, so that we shall not totally and finally apostatize. Third, He rescues us from evil by an ultimate deliverance, when He removes us to heaven.

"But deliver us from evil." This is a prayer, first, for Divine illumination, so that we may be able to detect Satan's devices (II Cor. 2:11). He who can transform himself into an angel of light (II Cor. 11:14) is far too subtle for human wisdom to cope with. Only as the Spirit graciously enlightens can we discern his snares. Second, this is a prayer for strength to resist Satan's attacks, for he is much too powerful for us to withstand in our own might. Only as we are energized by the Spirit shall we be kept from willfully yielding to temptation or from taking pleasure in the sins we commit. Third, it is a prayer for grace to mortify our lusts, for only to the degree that we put to death our own internal corruptions shall we be enabled to refuse external solicitations to sin. We cannot justly throw the blame on Satan while we give license to the evil of our hearts. Salvation from the *love* of sin always precedes deliverance from its *dominion*. Fourth, this is a prayer for repentance when we do succumb. Sin has a fatal tendency to deaden our sensibilities and to harden our hearts (Heb. 3:13). Naught but Divine grace can free us from unabashed indifference and work in us a godly sorrow for our transgressions. The very words "deliver us" imply that we are as deeply plunged into sin as a beast that is stuck in the mire and must be forcibly dragged out. Fifth, it is a prayer for the removal of guilt from the conscience. When true repentance has been communicated, the soul is bowed down with shame before God; there is no relief till the Spirit sprinkles the conscience afresh with the cleansing blood of Christ. Sixth, it is a prayer that we may be so delivered from evil that our souls are restored again to communion with God. Seventh, it is a prayer that He will overrule our falls for His glory and for our lasting good. To have a sincere desire for all these things is a signal favor from God.

What we *pray* for we must endeavor to *practice*. We do but mock God, if we ask Him to deliver us from evil and then trifle with sin or recklessly rush into the place of temptation. Prayer and watchfulness must never be severed from each other. We must make it our special care to mortify our lusts (Col. 3:5; II Tim. 2:22), to make no provision for the flesh (Rom. 13:14), to avoid every appearance (or form) of evil (I Thess. 5:22), to resist the Devil steadfastly in the faith (I Peter 5:8, 9), to love not the world, neither the things that are in it (I John 2:15). The more our character is formed and our conduct regulated by the holy Word of God the more we shall be enabled to overcome evil with good. Let us labor diligently to maintain a good conscience (Acts 24:16). Let us seek to live each day as though we knew it was our last one on earth (Prov. 27:1). Let us set our affection on things above (Col. 3:2). Then may we sincerely pray, "But deliver us from evil."

9

The Doxology

"For Thine is the Kingdom, and the power, and the glory, for ever. Amen" (Matt. 6:13).

This model for Divine worshipers concludes with a doxology or ascription of praise to the One addressed, evidencing the *completeness* of the prayer. Christ here taught His disciples not only to ask for the things needful to them, but to ascribe unto God that which is properly His. Thanksgiving and praise are an essential part of prayer. Particularly should this be borne in mind in all public worship, for the adoration of God is His express due. Surely if we ask God to bless us, the least we can do is to bless Him. "Blessed be the God and Father of our Lord Jesus Christ, who hath blessed us with all spiritual blessings in heavenly places in Christ!" exclaims Paul (Eph. 1:3). To pronounce blessing upon God is but the echo and reflex of His grace toward us. Devout praise, as the expression of elevated spiritual affections, is the proper language of the soul in communion with God.

The perfections of this prayer as a whole and the won-

drous fullness of each clause and word in it are not perceived by a rapid and careless glance, but become apparent only by a reverent pondering. This doxology may
be considered in at least a threefold way: (1) as an expression of holy and joyful praise; (2) as a plea and argument
to enforce the petitions; and (3) as a confirmation and
declaration of confidence that the prayer will be heard.
In this prayer our Lord gives us the quintessence of true
prayer. In the Spirit-indited prayers of the Old Testament Psalter, prayer and praise are continually joined
together. In the New Testament, the Apostle Paul gives
the following authoritative instruction: "Be careful for
nothing; but in every thing by prayer and supplication
with thanksgiving let your requests be made known unto
God" (Phil. 4:6). All the prayers of eminent saints, recorded in the Bible, are intermingled with the adoration
of Him who inhabits the praises of Israel (Ps. 22:3).

In this pattern prayer, God is made both the Alpha
and the Omega. It opens by addressing Him as our
Father in heaven; it ends by lauding Him as the glorious
King of the universe. The more His perfections are before our hearts, the more spiritual will be our worship
and the more reverent and fervent our supplications.
The more the soul is engaged in contemplation of God
Himself, the more spontaneous and sincere will be its
praise. "Continue in prayer, and watch in the same with
thanksgiving" (Col. 4:2). Is it not our failure at this point
that is so often the cause of blessing being withheld from
us? "Let the people praise Thee, O God; let all the
people praise Thee. *Then* shall the earth yield her increase; and God, even our own God, shall bless us" (Ps.

67:5, 6). If we do not praise God *for* His mercies, how can we expect Him to bless us *with* His mercies?

"For Thine is the Kingdom." These words set forth God's universal right and authority over all things, by which He disposes of them according to His pleasure. God is Supreme Sovereign in creation, providence, and grace. He reigns over heaven and earth, all creatures and things being under His full control. The words "and the power" allude to God's infinite sufficiency to execute His sovereign right and to perform His will in heaven and earth. Because He is the Almighty, He has the ability to do whatsoever He pleases. He never slumbers nor wearies (Ps. 121:3, 4); nothing is too hard for Him (Matt. 19:26); none can withstand Him (Dan. 4:35). All forces opposed to Him and to the Church's salvation He can and will overthrow. The phrase "and the glory" sets forth His ineffable excellency: since He has absolute sovereignty over all and commensurate power to dispose of all, He is therefore all-glorious. God's *glory* is the grand goal of all His works and ways, and of His glory He is ever jealous (Isa. 48:11, 12). To Him belongs the exclusive glory of being the Answerer of prayer.

Let us next notice that the doxology is introduced by the conjunction *for*, which here has the force of *because* or *on account of the fact that* Thine is the Kingdom, etc. This doxology is not only an acknowledgement of God's perfections, but a most powerful *plea* as to why our petitions should be heard. Christ is here teaching us to employ the *for* of argumentation. Thou art able to grant these requests, *for* Thine is the Kingdom, etc. While the doxology undoubtedly belongs to the prayer as a whole and is brought in to enforce all seven petitions, yet it seems to us to have a special and more immediate reference to the last one: "but deliver us from evil: *for* Thine is the Kingdom. . . ." O Father, the number and power of our enemies are indeed great, and they are rendered the more formidable because of the treachery of our own wicked hearts. Yet we are encouraged to implore Thy assistance against them, because all the attempts made by sin and Satan against us are really assaults upon Thy sovereignty and dominion over us and the promotion of Thy glory by us.

"For Thine is the Kingdom, and the power, and the glory." What *encouragement* is here! Two things especially inspire confidence towards God in prayer: the realization that He is *willing* and that He is *able*. Both are here intimated. That God bids us, through Christ His Son, to address Him as *our Father* is an indication of His love and an assurance of His care for us. But God is also the King of kings, possessing infinite power. This truth assures us of His sufficiency and guarantees His ability. As the *Father*, He provides for His children; as the *King*, He will defend His subjects. "Like as a father pitieth his children, so the Lord pitieth them that fear Him" (Ps. 103:13). "Thou art my King, O God: command deliverances for Jacob" (Ps. 44:4). It is for God's own honor and glory that He manifests His power and shows Himself strong on behalf of His own. "Now unto Him that is able to do exceeding abundantly above all that we ask or think, according to the power that worketh in us, Unto Him be glory in the Church by Christ Jesus throughout all ages, world without end. Amen" (Eph. 3:20, 21).

What *instruction* is here! First, we are taught to enforce our petitions with arguments drawn from the Divine perfections. God's universal kingship, His power, and His glory are to be turned into prevailing pleas for obtaining the things we need. We are to practice what Job sought to do: "I would order my cause before Him, and fill my mouth with arguments" (Job 23:4). Second, we are clearly directed to join petition and praise together. Third, we are taught to pray with the utmost reverence. Since God is so great and powerful a King, He is to be feared (Isa. 8:13). Hence it follows that we are to prostrate ourselves before Him in complete submission to His sovereign will. Fourth, we are instructed to make a full surrender and subjection of ourselves to Him; otherwise we do but mock God when we acknowledge verbally His dominion over us (Isa. 29:13). Fifth, by praying thus, we are trained to make His glory our chief concern, endeavoring so to walk that our lives show forth His praise.

"For ever." How marked is the contrast between our Father's Kingdom, power, and glory and the fleeting dominion and evanescent glory of earthly monarchs. The glorious Being whom we address in prayer is "from everlasting to everlasting . . . God" (Ps. 90:2). Christ Jesus, in whom He is revealed and through whom prayer is offered, is "the same yesterday, and today, and for ever" (Heb. 13:8). When we pray aright, we look beyond time into eternity and measure present things by their connection with the future. How solemn and expressive are these words *for ever!* Earthly kingdoms decay and disappear. Creaturely power is puny and but for a moment. The glory of human beings and of all mundane things vanishes like a dream. But the Kingdom and power and glory of Jehovah are susceptible to neither change nor diminution, and they shall know no end. Our blessed hope is that, when the first heaven and earth have passed away, the Kingdom and power and glory of God will be known and adored in their wondrous reality through all eternity.

"Amen." This word intimates the two things required in prayer, namely, a fervent *desire* and the exercise of *faith*. For the Hebrew word *Amen* (often translated "verily" or "truly" in the New Testament) means "so be it" or "it shall be so." This twofold meaning of supplication and expectation is plainly hinted at in the double use of *Amen* in Psalm 72:10: "And blessed be His glorious name for ever: and let the whole earth be filled with His glory; Amen, and Amen." God has determined it shall be so, and the whole Church expresses its desire: "So be it." This "Amen" belongs and applies to each part and clause of the prayer: "Hallowed be Thy name. Amen"—and so forth. Uttering the *Amen,* both in public and private prayers, we express our longings and affirm our confidence in God's power and faithfulness. It is itself a condensed and emphatic petition: believing in the verity of God's promises and resting on the stability of His government, we both cherish and acknowledge our confident hope in a gracious answer.

Scripture Index

Genesis
3:12—118
3:19—107
11:4—87
14:1-16—40
19:15-25—108
22:1—118
28:20—107
32:10—112
37, 39—58
50:14-21—116
50:15-21—40

Exodus
3:11—24
5:2—16
5:21—58
14:11—58
16:2—58
17:2—58
20:12—80
23:20, 21—73
34:5-7—84

Leviticus
19:17, 18—116

Numbers
12:3—23
12:13—40

Deuteronomy
29:29—100

I Samuel
8:5—58

16:7—46
24:1-22—41
26:1-25—41

II Samuel
11—125
12:13—114

I Kings
8:27—81
18:17—58
19:2—58
22:8—58

II Kings
20:12-19—120

I Chronicles
21:1—125
29:11—93

II Chronicles
32:31—120
37:27-31—120

Nehemiah
4—58

Job
22:21—53
23:4—133
33:24—114

Psalms
2:6—93
2:8—115

5:11—84
8:1—77
9:10—85
17:15—48
18:25—42
19:13—122
20:1—84
22:3—130
23:5,6—36
24:1—109
25:9—24
30:5—22
34:10—36
37:11—28, 29
37:16—29
37:21—40
40:12—19
42:1—34, 55
44:4—132
45:2—67
45:7—64
51:1—114
51:6—46
67:5,6—130, 131
69:4—114
69:12—66
69:29—62
72:10—134
78:41—118, 119
86:1—62
88:15—66
90:2—133
96:8—85
103:13—82, 132
103:20—104
104:27, 28—109

106:33—28
109:16—41
109:22—62
115:3—81
119:11—101
119:25, 28—102
119:27, 33—102
119:32, 36—102
119:53—20
119:117—120
119:136—96
121:3, 4—131
143:2—114
147:9—79
149:4—27

Proverbs
4:14—122
11:17a—42
14:21b—42
15:16—29
18:10—84
20:13—108
21:21—42
27:1—109, 128
30:8, 9—107
31:27—108

Ecclesiastes
9:10—97

Song of Solomon
2:15—122
5:16—61

Isaiah
6:2—103
6:6—103
8:13—133
9:6, 7—66
11:5—64
28:21, 22—15
29:13—133
35:10—22
45:8—32
45:11—85
46:10—100
46:12, 13—32
48:11, 12—131

50:6—66
51:5—32
53:3—62
53:11—67, 95
55:1—12
56:1—32
57:15—19
59:2—112
61:1—27
61:10a—32
64:6—12
64:8—79
66:1—81
66:2—19

Jeremiah
5:25—112
13:17—20
14:17—20
23:6—34, 64

Lamentations
1:12—63

Ezekiel
3:14—28
9:4—20
36:26—46

Daniel
4:30—87
4:35—100, 131

Hosea
2:9—109
14:2—75

Jonah
4:1—28

Micah
6:8—56
7:18—42

Haggai
2:8—109

Zechariah
9:9—64

Malachi
2:10—79
3:10—119

Matthew
3:2—11
4:1—121
4:17—11
5:1, 2—9
5:3—15 ff.
5:4—17 ff.
5:5—23 ff.
5:6—31 ff.
5:7—37 ff.
5:8—43 ff.
5:9—49 ff.
5:10-12—51, 52, 55 ff.
5:17—64
5:20—10, 34
6:7—75
6:9—72, 77 ff., 83 ff.
6:9-13—74
6:10—91 ff., 99 ff.
6:11—105 ff.
6:12—111 ff.
6:13—117 ff., 123 ff.,
     129 ff.
6:15—42
6:33—92
6:34—109
7:2—41
7:28, 29—9
11:5—12
11:19—63
11:27—67
11:29—13, 25
12:25-28—92
12:35—124
13:11—93
13:23—95
13:43—54
15:1-9—101
19:26—131
21:5—24
21:43—97
23:37—62
25:31-46—101
26:29—93

26:67—66
28:20—74

Mark
1:12—121
1:45—63
3:5—62, 96
4:11—93
7:24—63
7:34—62
15:34—63

Luke
1:35—65
1:53—36
2:49—64
4:29—66
6—10
6:46-49—101
7:30—100
7:41—113
9:58—62
10:27—94
11:2—72, 74
11:3—110
11:4—112
11:13—82
15:14—16
17:10—112
18:9-14—18
19:15—113
22:29—93
22:31-34—126

John
1:12, 13—95
1:17—15
3:3, 5—95
3:5—29, 93
4:34—64
5:17—93
5:24—115
6:15—63
6:48-58—12
6:50-58—29
7:2-10—64
8:48—66
8:50—65
8:59—66

11:35—62
12:14—64
12:27, 28—88
15:17-27—52
15:19, 20—59
16:14, 15—61
18:23—28
20:17—79

Acts
2:29-36—66
5:41—60
7:60—116
8, 9—57
8:22, 23—79
13:39—115
14:17—109
15:9—47
15:37-39—28
16:25—60
16:35-37—28
17:25-28—107
24:16—128

Romans
1:1—92
1:16—92
1:16, 17a—32
2:24—89
3:10—33
3:22-24—33
3:25—65
4:11—10
4:25—32
5:1—47
5:1, 2—115
5:3-5—59
5:19—33
6:13—96
7:14-24—96
7:21, 23, 25—44
7:24—20
7:24, 25—95
8:7—56
8:12—112
8:17—22, 30, 60
8:19—54
8:19-23—66
8:23—95

9:15—100
9:19—100
10:4—33
10:13-17—95
10:15—53
12:2—101
12:8—41
12:9—124
13:1-8—116
13:8—94
13:14—127
14:12—113
14:17—94, 97

I Corinthians
1:2—35
1:30, 31—35
2:9—36
4:20—93
7:5—125
10:31—89
13:9-12—48

II Corinthians
1:1—35
2:11—126
3:18—48
4:6—48
4:17—21
5:17—44
5:20—52
5:21—33, 65
6:10—21
7:10—18
8:9—62
9:7—41
10:4, 5—25
11:14—126

Galatians
1:4—124
4:6—80
5:22, 23—27
6:1—24
6:7b—41
6:10—108, 123

Ephesians
1:1—35
1:3—30, 79, 129

1:5—79
1:6—21
1:10—54
1:17—81
2:11-18—65
3:20, 21—132
4:2—25
5:14—121
5:18—35
6:1-3—80
6:11-18—121
6:15—53
6:16—124
6:18—123

Philippians
1:1—35
1:29—59
2:3—28
2:9-11—67
2:12, 13—35, 102
2:13—122
3:8-14—35
3:10—59
4:6—130
4:7—21, 35
4:10-14—94

Colossians
1:9, 10—104
1:13—93, 124
1:19, 20—53
1:20—65
2:13—114
3:2—128
3:5—127
3:16—92
3:17—97
4:2—130
4:12—104

I Thessalonians
4:3—101
5:22—122, 127

I Timothy
3:15—92
4:4, 5—107
6:6-10—94
6:8—107

II Timothy
1:16, 18—42
1:18—65
2:22—127
2:26—101
3:5—20
3:12—56

Titus
3:5—46, 65

Hebrews
1:3—93
2:17—65
3:13—127
5:7—63
6:4-6—95
7:22—114
7:26—65
10:9—64
10:22—47
10:32—95
10:34—60
11:6—78
11:24-26—24
11:25—60
12:1—20
12:11—21
12:14—94
12:23—95
13:8—133
13:20—53
13:20, 21—102

James
1:2, 3—121
1:13—118
1:14, 15—118

I Peter
1:14—54
1:19—65
2:19-24—58
2:20—59
2:22—65
3:15—87
4:2—101, 102
5:8—125
5:8, 9—127

II Peter
1:4—80
1:9—114
1:11—93
3:13—21, 30, 66, 94

I John
1:6-10—114
1:7—21, 44
1:8—43
2:13, 14—124
2:15—127
3:1—78
3:2—36
3:3—65
3:5—65
3:12—58, 124
5:14—73, 86
5:18, 19—124

Jude
21—42, 65

Revelation
4:11—100
5:8-14—103
7:15—103
11:15—93
12, 13—125
12:4—66
21:3, 4—22